Yacht and Small Craft Design

Yacht and Small Craft Design

From Principles to Practice

GORDON TROWER

Helmsman Books

First published in 1992 by
Helmsman Books, an imprint of
The Crowood Press Ltd
Ramsbury, Marlborough
Wiltshire SN8 2HR

British Library Cataloguing in Publication Data

A catalogue record for this book is available from the British Library.

ISBN 1 85223 709 0

Picture credits

Line-drawings and photographs by Gordon Trower

Acknowledgements

I should like to thank the following people for their help in the preparation of this book:
  My wife, Nola, for editing out the sillier parts from the manuscript, and for the days spent in the darkroom producing viable photographs from my somewhat dubious endeavours behind the Box Brownie.
  Steve Volz for proof-reading the first draft, before escaping to Spain.
  John Payne for proof-reading the final draft, until he broke his collar bone – a likely story!
  Henry Shaw, Computerman, for the printout in Fig 3.
  Tim Hope for the photographs in Figs 27, 64 and 130.
  Dave O'Shea for some planimetric assistance.
  Phil Samuel and Martin Beckett for posing – future modelling assignments gratefully accepted!

Typeset by Inforum, Rowlands Castle, Hants
Printed and bound in Great Britain by BPCC Hazells Ltd

Contents

CONTENTS

Introduction

Design is about designing. This may sound like a truism, but there are approaches to designing small craft which cannot really be called designing. It is possible to take an existing boat and base a design around it, perhaps with a few minor changes. This smacks of copying, a practice which we have been brought up to believe is deserving of a rap across the knuckles with a ruler.

At the other extreme, we can shun every boat ever designed and start with a clean slate, blank drawing film, or clear computer screen. This *tabula rasa* approach results in totally original design work, but is extremely demanding of underlying principles. The boat is a complex machine.

I like to think that effective design should have a strong sense of originality about it. But the extreme of total independence seems puritanical, and if boats are designed to the neglect of their evolution, something is missed. I believe that reference to existing, successful designs should therefore tend to follow rather than pre-empt new design work, if only as a verification or comparison.

Unless you have been locked away with your slate for the last twenty-five years, you cannot have failed to notice the impact which computers have made. These days, the boat can be draughted on a screen, modified readily towards a personal ideal, and the calculations can be completed in less time than it takes to find your slide rule.

If treated as a mere tool, the computer is a real aid to design. But computer software has reached a point now where one needs little understanding of design to produce a creditable final product. Instead of serving as a tool, the computer can become the master. The outcome, as I see it, is design without depth.

Just as I feel that one should resolve to design with minimal reference to other boats, so I believe that one should also develop an appreciation of the various factors relating to design, such as aerodynamics and hydrodynamics, before touching a keyboard, in order to avoid the superficiality which computers can create.

This book sets out to develop this appreciation as it applies to the boat and its components (with some emphasis on the sailing yacht). The systems (including computing) for producing the hull lines and their associated calculations are covered to extend the design factors allied to hull design. For completeness, the book culminates in a practical design procedure for those readers who like to put theory into practice.

Key to Symbols Used

A_{WP}	area of waterplane		l	characteristic length
a	area of cross-section or surface		p	pressure in a fluid
C_D	coefficient of drag		R_F	frictional resistance
C_F	coefficient of friction		Re	Reynolds number
C_L	coefficient of lift		s	sinkage
CI	common interval		SA	sail area
F_D	drag force		t	trim
F_H	heeling force		V	velocity of hull
F_L	lift force		VCB	vertical centre of buoyancy
F_R	driving force		VCG	vertical centre of gravity
F_T	total sail force		v	velocity of fluid
Fr	Froude number		$\textcircled{M}$	circular M
g	acceleration due to gravity		$\overline{V}$	volume of displacement
H	hull draught		ν	kinematic viscosity
h	height		α	angle of attack
LCB	longitudinal centre of buoyancy		λ	wavelength
LCG	longitudinal centre of gravity		ρ	density
LWL	length water-line			

Chapter 1

Creative Design

Dégas, the celebrated French artist, is famed for saying that a painter's most valuable work is produced only when he no longer knows what he is doing. A vision springs to mind of a hitherto capable boat designer working towards a state of blissful ignorance by undergoing psychoanalysis to help him forget his past. Perhaps you would be better not reading this or any other book on the design of small craft if you have any intention of putting its principles into practice!

I think Dégas meant that when the artist reaches a point of total familiarity with his medium he then can create without encumbrance. In fact, designers are used to creating – especially when their computer has just crashed!

Being paranoid about getting the calculations spot on gets in the way of the creative process. A confidence about acceptable error, an internalized judgement about the level of importance of some factor or other and an understanding of the principles which underpin the behaviour of small craft are critical to a creative approach to design.

Sitting all night on the weather deck of a yacht, racing a sailing dinghy in ghosting conditions, and powering a motor cruiser into a head sea are invaluable ways towards being a creative designer. I do not mean to imply that one all-night stint and one race and one cross-Channel trip provide the variety of experience necessary for the designer. Time of exposure is important, as a craftsman comes to know his tools and materials. Immersion in his subject is vital for the designer. The odd dunking in the drink probably helps, too.

A good number of years ago, a well-known designer's approach to design was used to sell a range of yachts. The advertisement, I recall, portrayed the designer looking out to sea from a headland, the caption reading 'This is the way Bob Miller designs yachts' or words to that effect. The message is an important one. There is virtue in looking out to sea as well as into VDUs if you want to combine science and 'feel' in your designing. Bob Miller went on to design an innovative Twelve Metre, based on research and analysis, which upset America's Cup history. You probably know him better as the late Ben Lexcen. The boat was *Australia II*. Perhaps we should all spend more time looking out to sea.

Pleasing proportion and visual balance are important ingredients of creative boat design just as they are in any other design work. It has been held that a design will look right only if it follows proportions or rules, such as, for the 'Golden Section'. In essence, it was regarded as a must that design and art should be built up from rectangular modules, the sides of which should have a fixed ratio (the 'Golden Ratio').

This ratio was a big secret held by the Ancients, which I am about to reveal: 1.618:1. Foolscap paper was in this ratio, so someone must have let out the secret already. What is good for the Parthenon ought to be good for a boat and so I present my masterpiece (*see* Fig 1). Such is my generosity that I give permission

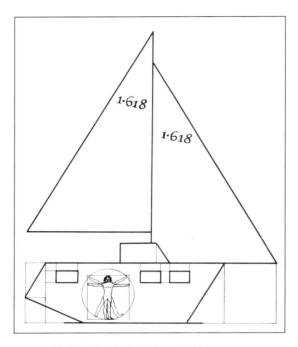

Fig 1 'Golden Section', designed with proportion in mind.

There are certain classic proportions which have evolved, particularly for yachts. The *sheerline*, which is the top edge of the hull as it runs fore and aft, is prominent and draws the eye. It has been suggested that yachts look better if the sheerline rises towards the bow from the lowest point about three-quarters of the length aft, then sweeps up at the stern by one quarter that of the rise forward (*see* Fig 2). A line which has a varying amount of curvature is usually thought to be more attractive than one which has a constant curvature, such as a segment of a circle.

There is a logic behind the shape of the conventional sheerline. The rising sweep forward inhibits water coming on deck, therefore keeping the boat drier. The hollow in the sheerline, known as the *sheer*, may look a little strange or exaggerated on a drawing or when the yacht is on a mooring, but when heeled this line appears straighter, due to the effect of the beam. In the same way, a straight sheer appears *hogged* when the yacht heels.

High freeboard (freeboard being the distance from the water-line at which a boat floats and the sheerline) gives the appearance of top-heaviness while low freeboard gives an impression of speed. But practicality tends to dictate. The requirement for seaworthiness militates against especially low freeboard. Also it is felt that the relative proportion of the superstructure (coachroof, cabin, doghouse) to the freeboard should not be too great, and in order to provide an appropriate amount of

for anyone to build this vessel without sending me a fee.

Preferences are dictated by fashion and familiarity. The fact that I prefer the shape of a sheet of A4 (ratio 1.414:1) to a sheet of foolscap does not mean that I could not be influenced to favour totally square paper next year. In the same way, our visual preferences for boats are not absolute; at least I do not think mine are.

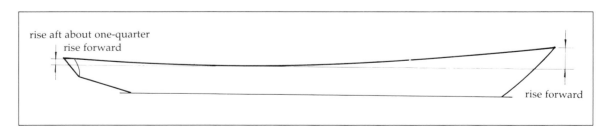

rise aft about one-quarter
rise forward

rise forward

Fig 2 Classic sheerline sweep.

Fig 3   Strong lines running fore and aft give an impression of reduced freeboard.

headroom down below the freeboard may be higher than otherwise desired. Various techniques are used by designers to make the freeboard appear lower, such as the use of bold divisions of colour on the topsides, 'go fast' stripes, and *knuckles* which create overhanging ledges in the topsides, running the length of the hull (*see* Fig 3). Some designers like broken sheerlines in order to minimize the freeboard except where it is necessary in the area of the accommodation (*see* Fig 4).

Small craft below about 8m (26ft) length overall are stretched (upwards) to provide standing headroom. If full standing headroom

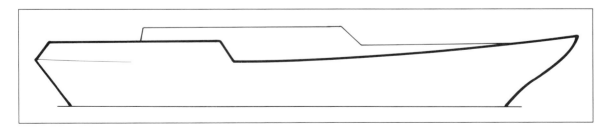

Fig 4   Broken sheerlines tend to be a matter of taste.

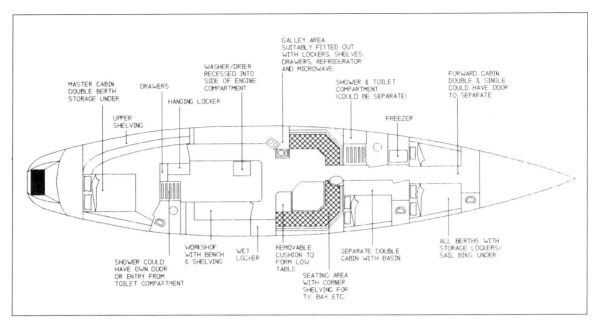

Fig 5   An outline accommodation plan of a 21.5m (70ft) boat to one of my designs. Drawn on computer, re-arranging the layout is simple. A low-cost, general purpose CAD program was used on a 386DX 20mHz PC compatible computer with maths co-processor and 24-pin dot matrix printer.

cannot be found, or the designer refuses to raise the superstructure line any higher, it often is preferable to design in bent-over headroom only. Headroom which is only a few centimetres short of one's skull is a real headache.

Of course, one man's headache is another man's backache, and the same problems of non-universal body proportions are evident when deciding on the positioning of backrests and chart tables. Anthropometrics (the study of the measurement of the human skeleton) forms the backbone of interior design. The discipline of ergonomics is concerned with efficiency in use. This means that the galley (more or less the kitchen), the heads (more or less the bathroom), and the other areas of the boat (more or less the living room and bedrooms) should be convenient to use, comfortable to be in and work efficiently (*see* Fig 5).

Anatomical models (*see* Fig 6) are excellent

Fig 6   Anatomical models can have headaches, too – not surprising with that hole in the head.

tools, and can be adapted to various positions. You can make your own out of card with paper fastener joints, to the same scale as your accommodation drawings (and don't forget the children).

With the strong emphasis on the visual and textural contexts which apply to boat interior design, it is no surprise that specialist designers have made a mark, particularly for larger luxury yachts, both power and sail. The discipline of interior design for the apartment is closely related to its equivalent at sea.

Perhaps we should employ exterior designers for the superstructure, since it also is influenced heavily by aesthetics. There should be a sense of harmony in the parts of the superstructure. Raked fronts give an impression of speed, which may be suitable for some craft and not others (*see* Figs 7 and 8). A sense of movement is conveyed by lines which progressively change their angle or spacing.

Sometimes, lines have a sense of rightness about them when they are parallel, and it may happen that to make lines look parallel, they should not be! The best approach seems to be to sketch, erase and sketch again, until the lines look right. Although I imply the use of a sketch-pad and pencil, computer graphics offer an alternative approach which avoids those annoying little grey rolls of eraser material that get everywhere.

Geometrical constructions can be used; for instance, the ends of the superstructure can be drawn so that if extended the lines all would meet at a focus (*see* Fig 9). But this is not intended as a prescription, because lines not following this principle can look equally or more effective.

Not that a designer should put all his energies into the profile. Boats are not cardboard cut-outs and it is necessary to visualize in three dimensions towards an integrated

Fig 7   The ultimate in raked coachroof fronts.

Fig 8   *The functionality of a forward raked wheel-house gives a sense of appropriateness for this small fishing boat.*

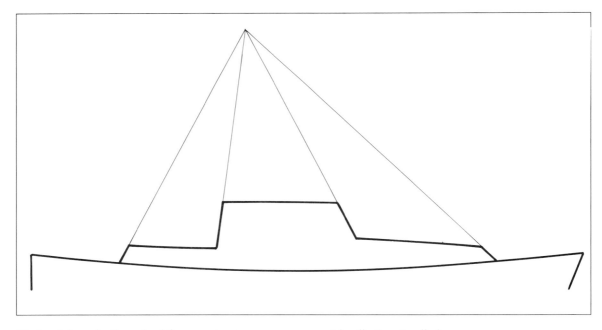

Fig 9   *A focus for the ends of the superstructure may or may not be effective visually because other factors are involved.*

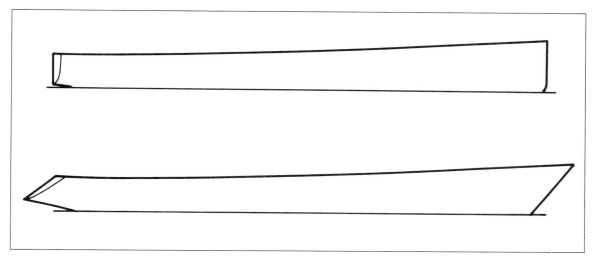

Fig 10   Bows should balance sterns.

whole. Such visualization takes practice, and the use of models and computer graphics techniques are not to be dismissed.

One tenet is that there should be an impression of balance. Visually, the boat should look, from any angle, as if it would balance somewhere around the middle, but rules of this kind are not to be regarded as immutable. Too great a symmetry in profile may give a sense of a lack of movement. It helps if boats look as if they are raring to go – bow first of course.

It is usually felt that the ends, that is the bow and stern, should express a similarity of form and volume. For example, plumb stems match plumb sterns and a long bow overhang should be coupled with a long stern overhang and a raked transom (*see* Fig 10). However, it is arguable whether aesthetic considerations should determine the shape of bow and stern, or play a significant part at all. Perhaps function should be the major determinant. This is the principal thrust of this book, though a capability in design does imply a developed visual awareness.

SUMMARY — CREATIVE DESIGN

1   Design work is enhanced by the designer developing a feel for and a confidence in his medium which should complement a scientific understanding in such a way that aesthetics and function are not regarded as disparate.

2   Rules relating to proportion, balance, harmony, movement, focus, colour and texture provide guidance for the designer, but probably are best not regarded as hard and fast.

Chapter 2

About Forces in Air and Water

Fluids and Pressure

Water is a liquid. Air is a gas. But when it comes to designing anything which floats, flies or dives, water and air have much in common and we think of them as *fluids*.

The water-skier sees little in common when he loses balance and finds himself skimming on a water surface which feels more like M1 than O$_2$. When he stops skimming and starts swimming, the water seems much friendlier, and more like air. Speed is important – go fast enough in air and it feels like lead shot.

We think of a fluid as something which *flows*. Water flows out of a dinghy's self-bailer; escaped gas from the cooking stove flows into the bilge and can be bucketed overboard (fluids can be a source of amusement too). However, it would be far-fetched to describe glass as a fluid even though it flows, albeit very, very slowly. This is called *creeping*. Old windows are thicker at the bottom than at the top, and if we could wait (or live) long enough, we would see the window end up as a puddle on the floor. Again, speed is important.

Sand has all the characteristics of a fluid; it can be poured from a container and it can be pumped just like water. Technically, sand is not a fluid because it consists of a large number of separate, solid particles. However, the behaviour of sand can be described as *fluidic*, and as such it serves as a useful model for understanding the behaviour of water and air.

Each particle of sand possesses mass, and when moving it therefore has *momentum*, which is a measure of unstoppability. When the particles impact a surface, a force is imparted which is more or less at right angles, or *normal*, to the surface. Fig 11 shows this force normal to the surface even where a particle strikes the surface with an angle of incidence. Lots of particles mean lots of force. Air and water have all these properties, but read molecules for particles. Remember, air is a fluid, and it really does have mass and momentum when it gets going, and can be pretty unstoppable.

The force which a fluid produces against a surface can be expressed in terms of *pressure*, which is the force occurring on each unit of area, such as a square metre, square millimetre, or square inch. The overall force on a thing in a fluid is assessed by the difference in pressure on its surfaces, affected by the relative velocity of the thing and the fluid. (Fast thing and still fluid is the same as still thing and fast fluid.)

Sometimes, relative velocity occurs when you least expect it. As you stare into your beer, it may come as a surprise that there is all manner of movement going on under the surface. Blowing off the head won't help you to see it. It has been speculated that your drink could move sideways ever so slightly, of its own accord. This has nothing to do with drinking too much beer, but hypothetically with the behaviour of 'beer' molecules. Since the molecules move in a random manner, it is supposed that a large number could at the

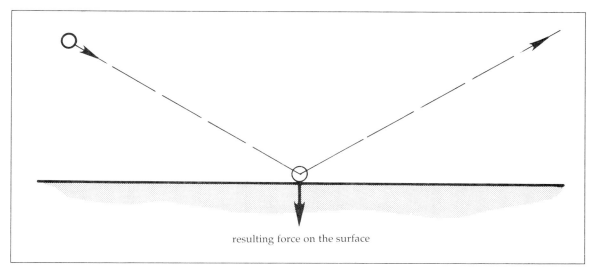

resulting force on the surface

Fig 11   The force is normal to the surface.

same instant move in the same direction, causing the most magnificent party trick of all time. This doesn't happen very often (but nor do magnificent party tricks).

The molecules keep themselves busy by continually running into each other (resulting in internal pressure) and into the wall of the glass (resulting in pressure on the sides and bottom). The pressure on the bottom of the glass is at its highest because the molecules are affected by gravity and there are large numbers bearing downwards. Drop a peanut in your beer and there will be more pressure on the peanut when it gets to the bottom of the glass than when it is at the top. As the peanut sinks, the beer flowing past it produces a zone underneath the peanut of raised pressure (from beer bombardment) and a zone above the peanut of lowered pressure, both of which slow its progress. Drop in a crisp and there will be pressure on its underside and none on the dry part (no beer here to produce pressure because the crisp floats).

The headline is that pressure differences produce forces, and that sinking savoury snacks spoil supping.

SUMMARY — FLUIDS AND PRESSURE

1   Under specific conditions, water and air behave similarly. Each is a fluid.

2   Fluids possess momentum when in motion. Pressure is increased when a fluid meets a body at its leading edge or surface, pressure always acting normally to the surface. Regions of low pressure also occur.

3   A force results where there is a difference in pressure around a body in a fluid, whether the fluid is static or in motion.

Fluid Phenomena

In the study of scientific matters, the term *phenomenon* is used to describe an event or occurrence. There need be nothing unusual or extraordinary about the happening, as is the case when we normally use the term. Although in true scientific tradition we can maintain an objectivity about the way fluids behave, there really is something phenomenal, or at least surprising, about what happens when fluids are in contact with three-dimensional shapes, known in scientific circles as *bodies*.

One of the most interesting of these phenomena is the *lift* produced on a body in a fluid stream, such as occurs in the case of an aircraft wing, hydrofoil, sail or propeller blade, all of which could be described as *foils*.

You can see by this that lift is not necessarily upwards. It is defined formally as that component of the total force, produced by the flow of fluid past the foil, which is at right angles to the flow, whether this is upwards, downwards or in any other direction.

The force, or component of force, in the line of the fluid flow is termed *drag* (*see* Fig 12). It is important to note that these directions are relative to the fluid's flow and not to the heading or centreline of the boat. Although the fluid is distorted as it travels past a body, lift and drag are regarded relative to the ambient flow, that is the general rather than the local flow direction.

It is not true to say that a body must be of aerofoil section as in Fig 12 in order to produce lift. A copy of Reed's *Nautical Almanac*, intended, of course, for navigation and other

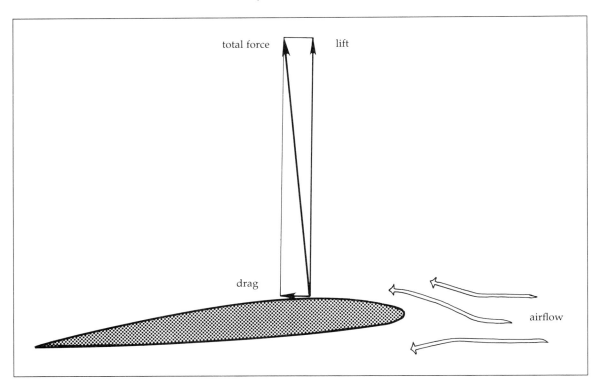

Fig 12   Lift and drag.

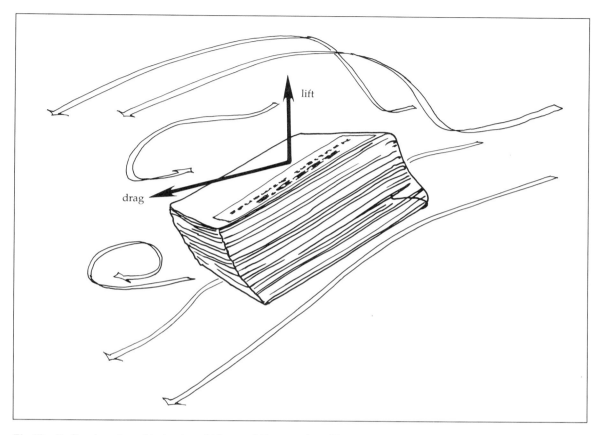

Fig 13   Bodies do not need to be shaped like aerofoils to produce lift.

purposes on board, rather than a lift device, nevertheless will produce lift when oriented to the air flow. The point is that, being somewhat obstructive in shape, it is not very effi- cient and more drag than lift results (*see* Fig 13). It can occur, of course, that a body possesses no lift at all but only drag, as in the case of a rudder in line with the water flow. In this

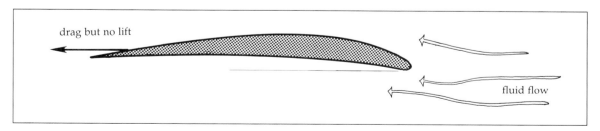

Fig 14   Drag but no lift.

case, its *angle of attack* would be zero. The copy of Reed's produces drag alone when its angle of attack is zero or ninety degrees, in which case we would expect symmetry in the airflow around it. But for asymmetrical aerofoils or hydrofoils, zero lift results at a negative angle of attack (*see* Fig 14).

In order to develop further the concepts of lift and drag and the way in which fluids produce forces on bodies, I present several examples.

Example 1: A Water Skier

It is first to be noted that no real buoyancy exists to support the skier; if the tow-boat stops, the skier sinks. Lift occurs because the water at high velocity impinges on the skis and is deflected backwards and downwards. The downward deflection indicates that lift occurs. This principle is shown in Fig 15 where a piece of aluminium sheet, formed to a ski shape, is pushed through sand. At the high velocity at which the skis operate, the behaviour of the water is very similar to that of the sand.

Essentially, high pressure is produced on the underside of the skis as a result of the bombardment of the surface by the water molecules. This can be viewed as a momentum effect (*see* Fig 16). The upturn at the front of the skis is able to deflect the water down-

Fig 15   Water and sand are alike when a skier is at high speed.

wards very sharply and stops them digging in, so the skier does not wave goodbye to the seagulls and say hello to the fish.

Upon starting, the skier presents the skis at a large angle to the water surface in order to produce the lift required at this low velocity. At speed, the angle of attack need only be low to provide lift equivalent to the weight of the person complete with skis.

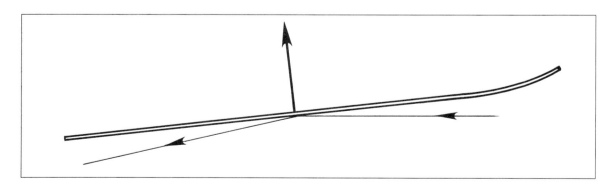

Fig 16   Water impacts the underside of the ski.

Example 2: An Anemometer

A very simple anemometer used to measure wind speed on the basis of rotational speed might consist of two cups which are fixed to an arm pivoted at its centre (*see* Fig 17). When presented to the wind, one cup produces more drag than the other because the air tends to accumulate, causing an increase in pressure. Momentum strikes again.

The two-cup arrangement described would not be very effective, quite apart from the undesirability of balancing the contents of the galley at the masthead! The use of three cups rather than two is preferable because this arrangement overcomes the null points when the arm is in line with the wind, and the design of the cups can be improved upon to give a greater turning moment (*see* Fig 18). In the position shown, the two cups produce lift as

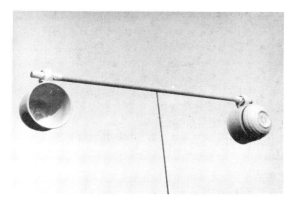

Fig 17   A very simple anemometer.

well as drag, and this results in a substantial turning force easily overcoming the drag of the third cup.

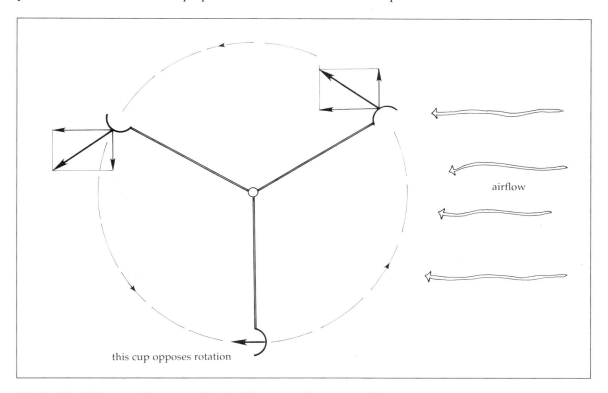

this cup opposes rotation

airflow

Fig 18   The lift force on the two cups is a significant contributor to rotation.

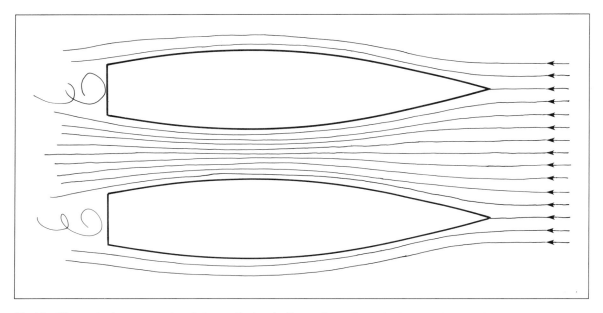

Fig 19   The venturi, or narrowing, between the two hulls speeds up the water to a greater extent than occurs on the outer side of the hulls.

Example 3: Two Yachts Moored Close Together

When two yachts are moored in close proximity in a tidal stream (*see* Fig 19) the yachts behave in what may seem an unpredictable manner. Instead of being pushed apart by the water, as one might expect, the yachts in fact move closer together. The breeches buoy, used to transport things and people from one ship to another, was introduced because of the danger of the ships closing on each other when steaming alongside.

The same phenomenon is observed if two balls, such as ping-pong balls, are suspended separately but in close proximity by lengths of thread and we blow through the gap. The balls move together until they nearly touch. Another, somewhat classic example, is demonstrated by blowing across the top of a sheet of paper, which causes the paper to lift. In each case, a force is produced towards the high velocity fluid stream. This is an important principle that

has a bearing upon the design of many aspects of marine craft, and demonstrates that an increase in velocity produces low pressure, the difference in pressure between one side of the body and the other resulting in a force towards the low pressure region.

Bernoulli and All That

I remember once, when I was younger, I saw a black and white horror film which promised the audience that a squealy siren would be heard whenever heads were about to roll. The principle which provides an explanation for *fluid dynamics* (relating to fluids in motion) is difficult to understand, and therefore I shall endeavour to provide a similar warning where necessary in order not to horrify the reader. Certainly, the principle which I intend to incant underpins many aspects of boat design.

SUMMARY — FLUID PHENOMENA

1   A body in a fluid stream experiences drag, which is defined as the force in line with the fluid flow. Lift may also be produced and is defined as the force at right angles to the flow.

2   The bombardment of a surface by particles of a fluid produces a force which can be explained in terms both of increased pressure and momentum. The force can be either drag alone or can be resolved into lift and drag.

3   Local increases in velocity of a fluid flowing past a body produce a reduction in pressure which commonly results in a significant lift force.

Daniel Bernoulli's spirit lives on in the theorem which he postulated over two hundred years ago. Its basis (squeal) is that the energy in a fluid system must remain constant within the system, and therefore if energy of one kind is reduced there must be a corresponding increase in some other energy form. This relationship is omnipresent.

Suppose you drop a marlinspike from the masthead while making a mess of checking the rigging. At the top of the mast the spike has stored energy of a sort, in that you have carried it up there. This energy, termed *potential energy*, is bestowed upon it because of its newly acquired high-level position in the world. Now, as the spike falls it loses potential energy. There is an equivalent gain in energy resulting from the spike travelling faster, this being termed *kinetic energy* (which is a function of the square of its velocity). The loss of both potential and kinetic energy is transformed into the energy of the spike (squeal) embedding itself, hopefully in the deck. This is a simplification which neglects such squealy matters as $E = mc^2$, global warming and entropy.

There are three forms of energy which Bernoulli's theorem describes. Two forms (already introduced) which the fluid can possess are kinetic energy (due to its movement) and potential energy (due to its height or change of height). The third (squeal) is the difficult one to grasp. It comes about from the pressure within the fluid, since it requires energy to create this pressure. This can be likened to the energy required to push a mass against a spring, thus compressing it.

My explanation so far is rather abstract. It helps to think of this principle of energy conservation with regard to a fluid flowing through a pipe of varying diameter which is badly plumbed and so rises and falls. As the pipe narrows, the fluid squeezes through a narrower gap, and in order that the same volume is passed in a certain time the fluid speeds up. Rivers do this sort of thing all the time. There is thus a gain in kinetic energy. Similarly, if the pipe rises there is a gain in potential energy. At any position along the pipe the sum of the energies will have a constant value.

This is expressed often by relating to the energies per unit mass at two positions, 1 and 2, along the pipe:

$$
\begin{array}{ccccc}
\text{pressure} & + & \text{kinetic} & + & \text{potential} \\
\text{energy} & & \text{energy} & & \text{energy} \\
\text{at 1} & & \text{at 1} & & \text{at 1}
\end{array}
$$

$$
\begin{array}{ccccc}
= & \text{pressure} & + & \text{kinetic} & + & \text{potential} \\
& \text{energy} & & \text{energy} & & \text{energy} \\
& \text{at 2} & & \text{at 2} & & \text{at 2}
\end{array}
$$

and mathematically (squeal):

$$\left(\frac{p_1}{\rho}\right) + \left(\frac{1}{2} \times v_1{}^2\right) + \left(g \times h_1\right)$$
$$= \left(\frac{p_2}{\rho}\right) + \left(\frac{1}{2} \times v_2{}^2\right) + \left(g \times h_2\right)$$

where the symbols relate to the properties of the fluid as follows:

p is the pressure, ρ (the Greek letter *rho*) is the density, v is the velocity, h is the height, g is more or less a constant at 9.81m/sec², being the acceleration due to gravity.

Very often, as far as the flow of air or water around parts of the boat is concerned, no change in the height of the air or water occurs and so the terms $(g \times h_1)$ and $(g \times h_2)$ can be omitted. (One exception is for the water flowing past the hull itself.) Expressing the energy level as constant, we have:

$$\left(\frac{p}{\rho}\right) + \left(\frac{1}{2} \times v^2\right) = \text{a constant.}$$

This can be expressed in terms of pressure by multiplying throughout by ρ, the density of the fluid, i.e.:

$$p + \left(\frac{1}{2} \times \rho \times v^2\right) = \text{another constant}$$

or:

static + kinetic = maximum pressure
pressure   pressure   within the system.

If by this stage you feel as if your brain has gone down the pipe along with the fluid, leaving an awful squealing alarm inside your head, then try Fig 20. I have tried to make it easy, resulting in a slight lack of precision.

The important message is that in the section of pipe which narrows, there is a reduction of the pressure within the fluid and acting on the inside of the pipe. Even if acceptable, this may

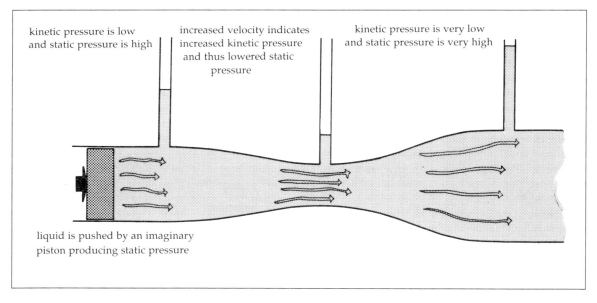

kinetic pressure is low and static pressure is high

increased velocity indicates increased kinetic pressure and thus lowered static pressure

kinetic pressure is very low and static pressure is very high

liquid is pushed by an imaginary piston producing static pressure

Fig 20   An increase in velocity in the venturi results in reduced static pressure.

SUMMARY — BERNOULLI AND ALL THAT

1   Bernoulli's theorem indicates that the total energy level of a fluid within a system must remain constant, and for changing conditions there will be an interchange of each of the forms of energy.

2   Each energy form can be considered in terms of pressure, and where no change in height of the fluid occurs, the maximum pressure within the system is the sum at any point of static pressure and kinetic pressure.

3   Kinetic pressure is expressed by ($\frac{1}{2} \times \rho \times v^2$). An increase in velocity in the vicinity of a body increases kinetic pressure, signifying a decrease in static pressure indicative of the production of a force.

---

seem somewhat mind-boggling because it is as if the fluid is being squeezed into the venturi and therefore that pressure should increase. But the observable phenomenon, cited in 'Fluid Phenomena', is that two yachts in a tidal stream move closer together, signifying a reduction in pressure where velocity increases. Although blowing across the top of a Reed's *Nautical Almanac* will not cause it to rise (because of its weight), the high velocity and hence low pressure effect is noted for the lighter sheet of paper which successfully 'defies' gravity.

The connection between high velocity and low pressure is generally thought to be causative in the sense that high velocity produces low pressure. It may help the reader's penny to drop to think of low pressure producing high velocity, as occurs in a weather system where low barometric pressure results in strong winds. It's just like sucking, really.

Calculating Bernoullian Forces

The reader would be forgiven for wondering why the last section seemed to be leading towards the design of a boat's plumbing. Despite the preoccupation with fluid flow in pipes, the flow around sails, rigging or rudders can be thought to be in the form of a series of pipes of rectangular section, each one joined to the next. Each pipe (or its cross-section) can be thought to be a *streamtube* and the walls of the pipes *streamlines* (see Fig 21).

The streamtubes are formed by the streamlines, each streamline being defined by the path of a single particle of the fluid. In flowing past a body in the fluid stream, the path of the particle, and therefore the streamline, is distorted accordingly. One streamline can be chosen which, at least theoretically, meets the body in such a way that the particle has no tendency to move to either side of the body. This is termed the *stagnation* streamline.

For predictive purposes, realistic streamlines can be constructed fairly easily around bodies if no allowance is made for any breakdown of the flow, such as occurs when the flow breaks down around a foil, or when a *wake* is formed, this being the eddying flow behind the body. For a streamlined form at a small angle of attack, there may be little flow disruption. Therefore, the assumption made of *streamlined flow*, as it is called for an *ideal fluid*, is reasonable. For an obstructive shape, such as a cylinder or a nautical almanac, streamlined flow is not representative.

Streamlines can be constructed by a trial

25

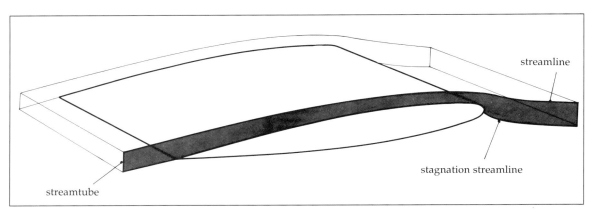

Fig 21   A streamtube defined by streamlines which are assumed not to distort laterally.

and error method, assuming streamlined flow, the object being to draw the streamlines such that 'squares' are formed as shown for the cylinder in Fig 22. Electrical analogue and computer techniques provide better systems for the construction of streamlines around foils.

The point of the exercise is that it does offer a prediction of the changes in velocity which occur in the vicinity of a foil. For instance, if a streamtube narrows to one-third its initial width, the local fluid velocity would be three times greater. Bernoulli's theorem permits the

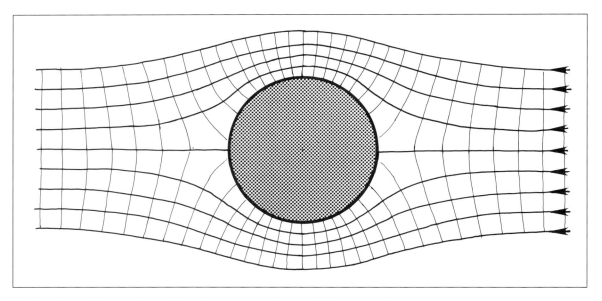

Fig 22   Streamlines are sketched by judgement and then verified by attempting to construct 'squares'. Streamlines more closely spaced would enable more accurate squares to be constructed close to the body. The method is not applicable to fluids which are not ideal.

SUMMARY — CALCULATING BERNOULLIAN FORCES

1 Streamlines constructed around a body or foil indicate the local velocity based upon the width of the streamtube, and provide a theoretical means of determining the force produced assuming streamlined flow.

2 More practically, the model of a foil is tested to obtain its lift and drag characteristics. The predicted lift and drag forces for the full-sized foil is obtained from an adaptation of Bernoulli's theorem in the general form $F = \frac{1}{2} \times \rho \times a \times v^2 \times M$, where M is a multiplication factor specific to the foil, the flow conditions and whether lift or drag is sought.

determination of the pressure at different points, from which is found the force over sections of the foil. By summing these, taking account of both surfaces, the total force is derived.

It is of value for the designer to be able to predict how much side force a keel generates or the amount of lift a hydrofoil produces. But the manual construction of streamlines is not reliable and certainly is tedious (and not everyone has an analogue field plotter in their garden shed). Nevertheless, an appreciation of streamlines underpins the understanding of foil performance.

Good results are obtained, in fact, by testing models of the full-sized form in order to establish its characteristics. Alternatively, standard data are used. For example, if one designs a keel using a standard section (the section being the shape of a horizontal cutting plane) its quantitative lift and drag properties are known as a result of previous testing. These properties can then be related to the keel in question to give the predicted lift and drag for its area, outline shape, angle of attack and the water velocity over it.

Bernoulli's theorem comes to our rescue in making the connection between the standard data and the predicted lift and drag. This theorem makes the assumption of streamlined flow. The presumption is that no energy is lost and this requires that there is neither friction of the fluid against the surface nor between

'layers' of the fluid as they slide one over the other. Under this condition, the kinetic pressure is indicated to be $(\frac{1}{2} \times \rho \times v^2)$. We can think of this in balance with the static pressure which represents the force produced per square unit of area. It follows that the force, either total, lift or drag, relates to the product of pressure and area, i.e. $(\frac{1}{2} \times \rho \times v^2 \times a)$.

There does need to be a multiplication factor made to allow for the realities of the form in the fluid flow, to serve as a 'fudge' factor. Also the multiplication factor must take into account whether we wish to predict either lift or drag. The nature of this factor will be covered at length when dealing with drag and lift. For the time being, we can say that the force on a body in a fluid stream is given by:

$$F = \frac{1}{2} \times \rho \times a \times v^2 \times M,$$

where M symbolizes the multiplication factor. This formula is a fairly universal one and is used extensively in the calculation of fluid forces necessary for ensuring that a boat will perform as expected.

Drag on Wholly Immersed Components

The explanation for the drag of a boat's hull as it moves through the water is guided by the same principle which underpins the drag on bodies which are totally immersed in a single

Fig 23   High drag despite a streamlined form to the superstructure.

Fig 24   A highly obstructed mast.

fluid. But there is a major difference in that the hull is affected by the interface of water and air. In fact, it is not the presence of air which is of significance, but only that the water due to gravitational influence produces a surface. This surface distorts in the form of waves as the hull moves through it and these waves feature as a major factor in a consideration of the hull's drag. It is my intention to reserve hull drag, or resistance as it is generally known, for a later section.

The kinds of body which count as fully immersed in either air or water, and therefore do not produce surface waves, are, for example, coachroofs, deck hardware, rigging, masts, keels, sacrificial anodes, propeller bracketry

(and the propeller itself for a yacht when sailing) (*see* Figs 23, 24, 25 and 26). Human bodies also count as immersed bodies, hopefully being surrounded totally by air. Drag on everything under the water is bad news.

Above the water it is mostly bad news, and this is why the skipper often demands that the crew present as little windage as possible by keeping low rather than standing up unnecessarily on deck. The good news is when the wind is from behind and then those baggy waterproofs and that massive superstructure actually pay off. But generally, drag is a drag.

Sometimes a high level of drag is sought, such as for a sea anchor to keep a boat's bow into the wind in storm conditions, or the blade

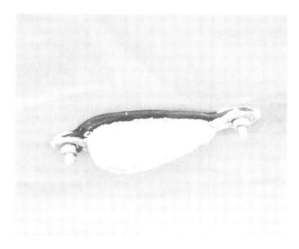

Fig 25   The faired shape of this sacrificial anode is negated largely by the fastenings.

of an oar in order to propel a skiff as effectively as possible. Both are relatively obstructive to the water in comparison with, for example, the lead bulb on the bottom of a keel, a means of concentrating weight as low as possible (*see* Fig 27).

For a thin, streamlined form such as the keel itself or the rudder, drag is small. If we utilize a plate of little thickness for the keel or rudder, then drag will be lower still, although this is neither a practical nor hydrodynamically satisfactory solution. The very thin plate would be inadequately strong, and because water flow tends to break down readily when the plate is angled to the water flow, it is an inferior producer of lift. However, no matter how thin the plate, it will still exhibit drag

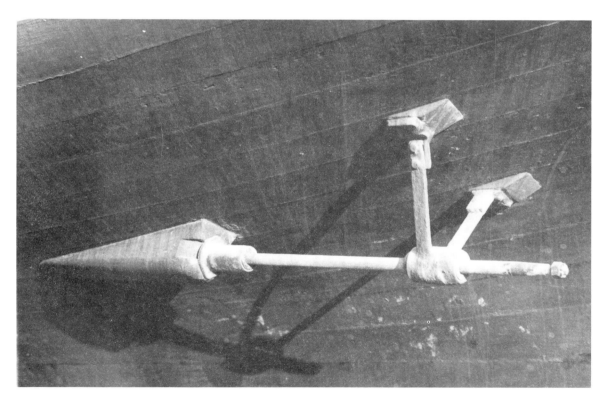

Fig 26   Propeller bracketry can be of high drag, particularly when off-centre and not shielded by the keel.

Fig 27   A bulbed keel.

even when aligned with the water flow, due to what is referred to as *frictional drag* of the water as it slides past the plate. For most shapes, their obstructiveness produces a more significant element of drag. This component is termed *form drag*.

In flowing past a body, the fluid experiences velocity changes. Typically the fluid slows when it meets the leading edge, then speeds up, and finally slows again, having passed the body. The reduction in the velocity in the direction of flow when the fluid first meets the body is indicative of a momentum change and hence a force is produced. At the aft end of the body the molecules of the fluid endeavour to fill the space which the aft end of the body tries to create, producing lowered pressure.

So both the raised pressure at the leading edge and the lowered pressure at the trailing edge contribute to overall drag. The extent and nature of the streamlining of the fore and aft sections will affect the proportion of drag which each contributes. For a flat plate presented at 90 degrees to the flow, tests have shown that the front face generates 70 per cent and the rear face 30 per cent of the total drag.

A means of measuring the extent or effectiveness of streamlining is via the *coefficient of drag*. In recent years this term has gained currency in the marketing of cars as the need for low-drag car bodies for improved fuel economy has increased. Generally, a coefficient provides a means of relating one thing to another or as a multiplier to account for particular properties. Although it lacks rigour, the coefficient of drag of a body can be regarded as the drag relative to that of a flat plate of the

Fig 28   A small wind tunnel.

same cross-section. This presumes no change in fluid or velocity, and that the flat plate is presented square to the fluid flow.

It follows that two bodies, such as keel bulbs, of the same shape but of different sizes would have the same coefficient of drag. The actual drag of the larger bulb would of course be greater, approximately in proportion to its cross-sectional area. For instance, if one bulb were twice the size of the other, its cross-sectional area would be four times greater, and it would have correspondingly four times the drag at the same speed. However, it has to be said that this is a modelling of a situation which is not totally accurate (as is so often the case in the real world application of mathematics).

This principle is applied, with a little more sophistication, to the prediction of drag using physical models. The model is shaped to scale

and its drag measured in a wind tunnel (*see* Fig 28), water channel (*see* Fig 29) or tank. This enables the coefficient of drag to be deduced. It is to be noted that its value is empirical, that is, derived by experimentation. The drag of the full-sized form can then be predicted by assuming the same coefficient of drag. Good results can be obtained at minimal expense, but the value of the prediction does rest upon how similar are the flow conditions around both the model and the full-sized form. In order to obtain this condition, termed *dynamical similarity*, the velocity of the fluid flow past the model will have to be different from that of the full-sized form. It may even be necessary to use a different fluid for testing.

Testing of full-sized mock-ups avoids the difficulties imposed by dynamical similarity. Although feasible as a means of testing the air resistance of a hull and deck, wind tunnels are

Fig 29   And a small water channel. The drag of different fairings around a simulated opening in the hull is being tested, the water flowing from right to left.

not large enough to test the rig of a yacht, except at model size. Cars can be tested in a wind tunnel, and this has led to something of a revolution in their shapes, in that they have become far more aerodynamic.

However, it is too easy to overlook the fact that the coefficient of drag does not provide a direct measure of drag. Sub 0.3 values may seem impressive for a large family saloon, particularly when compared with the brick-like aerodynamics of a Mini, which tests at around 0.42. But the Mini is likely to have the

---

SUMMARY — DRAG ON WHOLLY IMMERSED COMPONENTS

1   The drag of a body totally immersed either in water or air can be split into form drag and frictional drag.

2   Form drag results from both the raised pressure of the forebody and the lowered pressure of the aftbody. Frictional drag occurs as a result of the fluid flowing over the surface.

3   The coefficient of drag provides an assessment of the degree of streamlining. A model's coefficient of drag can be found from testing, which then enables the drag of the full-sized form to be predicted, given the condition of dynamical similarity.

lesser drag at the same speed because its cross-section or projected area is substantially less.

Form Drag and Flow Conditions

An 'ideally streamlined' body has a coefficient of drag of about 0.04 – considerably less than the bottom limit achieved for any car. Fig 30 indicates typical coefficients of drag derived by testing for a variety of forms. These values can be used to calculate the drag occurring on a body of the same form. For example, if we wish to predict the drag on a length of rod rigging we can assume a coefficient of 0.9 because its shape is cylindrical.

Suppose the rod rigging is 8m long and 6mm (that is 0.006m) in diameter, the wind velocity is 10m/s (nearly 20 knots) and the density of the air is taken to be 1.225kg/m³ (which means that one cubic metre of air has a mass of 1.225kg). The formula stated to determine the force acting on a body in a fluid stream was:

$$F = \tfrac{1}{2} \times \rho \times a \times v^2 \times M$$

where M is a multiplication factor to allow for the efficiency or otherwise of the body and the flow conditions. In connection with drag, this factor is in fact the coefficient of drag C_D. Note that a is the area of the cross-section as presented to the fluid, the determining of C_D from testing being based on this assumption.

From the example, we see that:

$$a = 8 \times 0.006 = 0.048\text{m}^2.$$

Since the drag force is given by the formula $F_D = \tfrac{1}{2} \times \rho \times a \times v^2 \times C_D$, we can find the drag. This is measured in newtons (abbreviated to N; there are nearly 10N in 1Kg) provided all

Fig 30   For a fluid flowing towards each of the bodies depicted, the coefficient of drag would be approximately 0.90, 0.35, 0.05, 0.55, 1.15 (left to right).

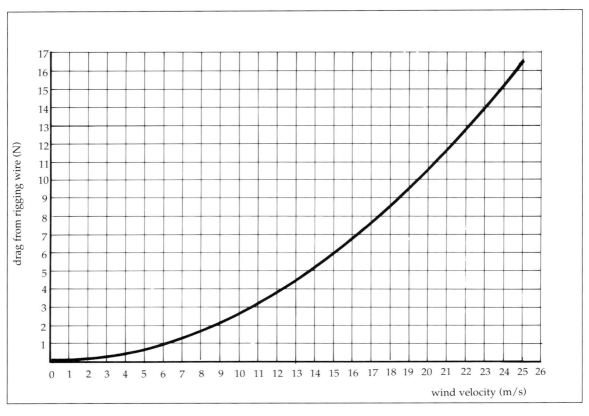

Fig 31 Rigging drag against wind speed. At the highest ever recorded wind velocity of 103m/s (201 knots), drag would be 283N (64lb) for this length of wire.

measurements are in metres, seconds and kilograms. Thus:

$$F_D = \frac{1}{2} \times 1.225 \times 0.048 \times 10^2 \times 0.9 = 2.646N.$$

For those readers who struggle with the metric system, this is about 0.6lb. (Still don't like decimals? Try 9½oz.) As an aside, it was tradition in aerodynamics when using the imperial system to measure the mass of bodies in what were called, unbelievably, *slugs*. Imperially speaking, the drag should be expressed as lbs-force, or it could be expressed in *poundals*. But enough of this nostalgia.

A graph of the drag from the length of rigging against wind speed is shown (*see* Fig 31).

Significant is the way in which drag increases with wind speed. In fact, a doubling of the wind speed produces a fourfold increase in the drag. From the graph it is seen that in 25m/s (48.5 knots) of wind the drag on this single shroud is about 16.5N (3.7lb). Multiply that a few times for all the shrouds, stays and flag halyards, add on the various other elements of parasitic drag, including hull windage, and it is easy to see why yachts do not like sailing to windward in these conditions. Tacking can become impossible.

Although the graph provides a reasonably sound model for the drag of a wire, it does presume that the coefficient of drag remains

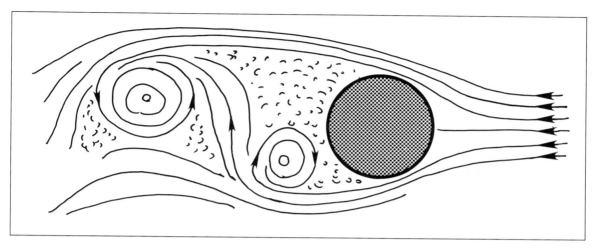

Fig 32   Vortex streets around a cylinder.

constant. In practice, it varies at different speeds according to the flow conditions which occur. It is possible that C_D could range between about 0.7 and 1.3 depending upon the kind of wake formed.

At extremely low speeds – sub-ghosting wind speeds for sailing craft – the coefficient of drag may lie outside these limits. With a sufficiently low air velocity, the flow around the shroud would be wholly *laminar*, the same as for streamlined flow, and no wake would be present. The addition of a fairing would not reduce C_D any further. Just a little higher a wind speed and C_D shoots up to very high values, but again this is below the practical wind speed range. Lest you should start suffering sleepless nights wondering about how to overcome this seeming inefficiency, rest assured that C_D stabilizes to more normal values at wind speeds (for this shroud) above 0.01m/s (¹⁄₅₀ of a knot).

For most of the wind speed range, the C_D of the shroud is 0.9 to 1.0. Under these conditions, the flow is not particularly admirable and *vortex streets* are produced (*see* Fig 32). The manner in which vortex streets are formed around tall buildings keeps architects awake at night. At certain speeds the vortices

are shed and re-established alternately on each side of the building, thus producing alternating forces which make the occupants feel as if they are at sea. Shrouds on yachts do vibrate and hum worryingly.

If the wind velocity were around 1200m/s (2300 knots!), which is quite a few parsecs off the Beaufort scale, then the flow around the shroud is impressive, (*see* Fig 33). Even more impressive is C_D which reduces to about 0.3. Actually, it picks up again at higher speeds still to about 0.35, gradually falling back again at the kinds of wind speeds that would blow us off the face of the Earth. It is not true to say that these high speeds are necessary to obtain the condition of a low C_D, since this applies to this particular example of the shroud, which has a small diameter. Given a larger diameter, then the peculiarity of low C_D is feasible within a normal range of wind speeds.

The two factors of velocity and diameter are wrapped up in *Reynolds number*, symbolized by *Re* (or *Rn*). Diameter is an expression of *characteristic length* and is measured in the line of the fluid flow. Reynolds number provides a framework for assessing the flow conditions of a fluid around a body, and therefore some

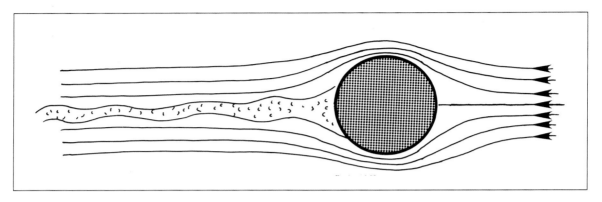

Fig 33   High speed produces a lesser wake, though at 1200m/s the 8m long by 6mm diameter shroud produces a theoretical drag of 12 701N (1¼ tons)!

account needs to be made of the fluid itself. Of importance is the measurement of the fluid's *kinematic viscosity*, which is its viscosity relative to its density. Kinematic viscosity is standardized for water and for air. Reynolds number is determined by:

$$Re = \frac{vl}{v}$$

where v is the fluid's velocity, l is the characteristic length of the body and v (the Greek letter *nu*) is the kinematic viscosity (0.0000146 for air and 0.0000114 for water – don't worry about the units).

You may have picked up the idea that Professor Osborne Reynolds was not afraid of awkward numbers. You would be right. Reynolds number for the 6mm diameter shroud (l = 0.006m) at a velocity of 10m/s (19.4 knots) in air is calculated to be $Re = 4110$ (which can be expressed as 4.11×10^3). But mostly the various parts of a boat operate at higher Reynolds numbers than this, the range of 10^4 to 10^6 being common.

Of great interest as far as design is concerned is the possibility that the flow condition can be modified to achieve lower C_D values over a wider range, in particular at lower speeds. Earlier this century, Ludwig Prandtl demonstrated this by a classic experiment. He used smoke to show the wake that was formed when air flowed past a sphere. When smooth, the sphere exhibits a large wake with *separation* occurring even before the point of maximum diameter. But when Prandtl attached a wire just upstream of the point at which separation occurred with the smooth sphere, the wake was reduced dramatically. This occurred at a *critical* Reynolds number of about 4×10^5.

The wire caused the air to re-attach itself to the sphere, at least temporarily. This simulated the wake formation occurring at higher speeds, when the addition of such a trip-wire is unnecessary. The reduction in C_D by about two-thirds signifies the same proportionate reduction in drag. Doubtless, it seems surprising that a surface with deliberate interference can result in less drag. Inducing turbulence works well for a golf ball. The modern dimpled golf ball can be driven four or five times further than its smooth predecessor, although, to some extent, this results from the enhancement of lift which the dimples provide when the ball rotates.

Before designing in dimples to every part of the boat, it has to be said that this is a special

---

SUMMARY — FORM DRAG AND FLOW CONDITIONS

1 Form drag is given by $F_D = \frac{1}{2} \times \rho \times a \times v^2 \times C_D$. The coefficient of drag is a function of cross-sectional area and varies according to the fluid's flow conditions which can be assessed by Reynolds number, defined by $Re = \dfrac{v \times l}{\upsilon}$.

2 At very low values of Reynolds number, fluid flow is essentially streamlined, even for obstructive shapes. At a critical Reynolds number of about 4×10^5, the flow separates prematurely, producing an exaggerated wake and a large coefficient of drag.

3 Turbulence inducers can reduce the coefficient of drag substantially under critical Reynolds number conditions such that the fluid is 'tripped' so that it re-attaches to the surface.

---

case, the golf ball being obstructive in shape. The dimples, as a tripping device, do not need to cover the entire surface. It is feasible that many components on boats, such as masts (*see* Fig 34), would benefit from the artificial creation of turbulence and this depends upon the Reynolds number of the air or water as it flows past the component.

Lift Produced by Aerofoils and Hydrofoils

Amongst those involved with aircraft, there is much talk about lift, which is not unreasonable since this is useful for keeping aircraft where they belong. Much research conducted on behalf of the aerospace industry has produced results and prescriptions borrowed by the designers of boats. The fact that aircraft are intended to get no wetter than from a heavy shower does not invalidate the data available. The key which enables us to use aircraft data to design our keel, for example, lies in Reynolds number. Provided we ensure a similarity of Reynolds number, the flow conditions will also be similar.

When air or water flows past a foil (*see* Fig 35), the fluid moving over the upper surface

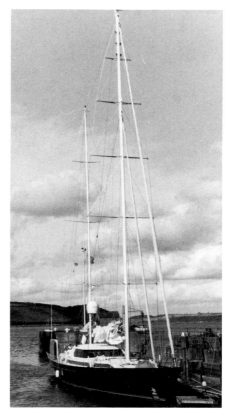

Fig 34 Large yachts require complex rigging systems, with an attendant high windage penalty.

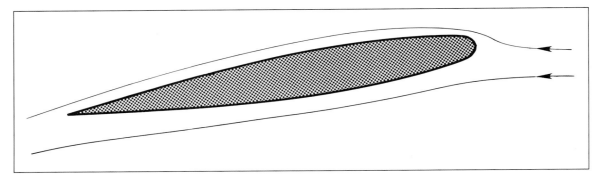

Fig 35   Relative distance around a foil.

travels a greater distance than that over the lower surface. The fluid on the upper surface must therefore be at higher velocity and this means that the pressure in this region is lowered, following Bernoulli's theorem. On the lower surface the fluid slows, resulting in an increase in pressure. The consequential forces acting on the wing (foil) produce lift.

The variations in velocity around the foil produce a force distribution as shown (*see* Fig 36). If the foil were a kite it would be high flying, the string supporting it following the

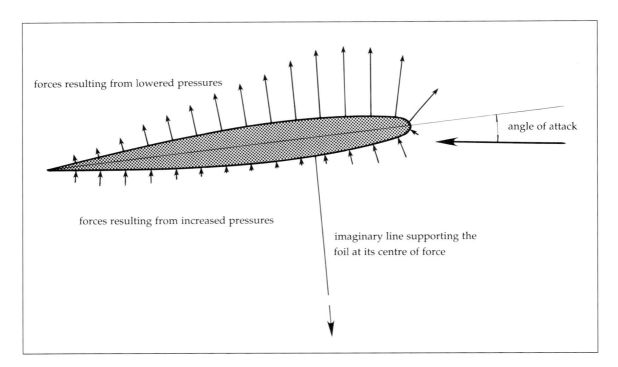

Fig 36   Aerodynamic force distribution and centre of force.

line shown. The string produces a force equal and opposite to the aggregate force on the kite, which it is noticed is about 25 per cent aft of the leading edge, though this position varies with the angle of attack and the shape of the foil. This position can be described as the *centre of force*.

It is reasonable to suppose that if we improve the relative velocities of the upper and lower surfaces, lift improves. The concept of *circulation* is used often to describe this phenomenon as a general explanation for various lift producing systems. Relative to the idealized fluid flow, there is a 'movement' forward on the underside (reduced velocity) and aft on the upper surface (increased velocity), thus indicating a circulation. It might be thought that we could maximize circulation and therefore lift by using a helmet-type form (*see* Fig 37). But the flow is not sustained over the upper surface, and therefore neither is the high velocity hoped for because of the substantial distance over the top of the helmet. Motorcyclists are not lifted off the saddle.

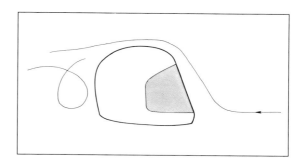

Fig 37   Separation occurs.

In a similar fashion, increasing the angle of attack of a conventional foil produces a breakdown of flow, termed *stalling*, which results in a loss of lift (*see* Fig 38). But the lift resulting from the high pressure on the underside actually increases with larger angles of attack up to about 45 degrees.

Whether a foil is to be designed for a flowed, partially flowed, or stalled state affects the *planform* (the outline shape of the foil). For the foil at a small angle of attack and

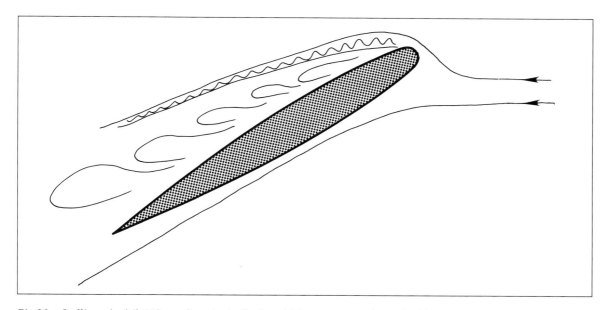

Fig 38   Stalling of a foil. Lift results principally from high pressure on the underside.

with attached flow, the force distribution (*see* Fig 36) indicates that the most useful area of the foil is towards the front. To look at it another way, we could remove the aft part without a monstrous loss. Area for area, the most efficient foil is one which is long and narrow. This feature is taken to an extreme with some gliders, whose wing span is limited only by the structural difficulties of sticking on the wings.

At larger angles of attack, the best defence is a foil which is relatively short for its width since the underside forces start to dominate. An aircraft produces more lift at take-off when the angle of attack is high if it has short wide wings, in complete contrast to the glider.

A more elegant way of describing the planform proportions of a foil uses the term *aspect ratio*. This, formally, is the ratio of the distance, measured along the foil perpendicular to the flow, to the average length measured in the line of the fluid flow. Thus gliders have wings of very high aspect ratio, and water-skis are of very low aspect ratio. (Think about that for a moment.)

Much theoretical work on foils is based upon the assumption of infinite aspect ratio, which results in two-dimensional flow only, i.e. back and forth, up and down, but not sideways. Allowance then must be made for the behaviour of the fluid around the end or ends of the foil, which does result in a loss of efficiency. Because the top surface of a wing is at lower pressure than the bottom surface, the fluid claws its way upwards around the ends. This effect produces vortices which are visible from the ends of the wings of aircraft under certain conditions of heat haze. There are various ways of minimizing this inefficiency, some of which will be considered later.

The lift produced by a foil depends upon the planform area (the larger the area, the more the lift), the fluid (water produces more lift than air), the velocity (the higher the velocity, the more lift) and the form and pro-

portions of the foil. The shape of the foil is defined by its section, aspect ratio and plan form. The *coefficient of lift* is a function of these factors, together with the angle of attack. Although a stab can be made at its value, the coefficient of lift is derived more exactly from experimentation. This involves setting up a foil of known area at a chosen angle of attack and measuring the lift force resulting from air or water flowing past at known velocity.

The coefficient of lift is a measure of the lifting effectiveness of the foil, that is, how well the foil operates as a lift producer. Just like the coefficient of drag, the coefficient of lift has no units because it is used for comparative purposes and for calculations when it serves as a multiplier. Coefficient of lift can be low but may be as high as three, depending upon the nature of the foil or foil combination and the angle of attack.

Once the coefficient of lift for a foil is established by experimentation, we then can deduce the actual lift a foil of similar form would have at the same angle of attack. Suppose the coefficient of lift C_L at an angle of attack of 3 degrees is 0.4 and we wish to calculate the lift in fresh water (density 1000 kg/m³) flowing at 15m/s (29.1 knots) of a similar foil having a surface area of 0.8m² (8.6ft²). Using Bernoulli's theorem:

$$F_L = \tfrac{1}{2} \times \rho \times a \times v^2 \times C_L$$
$$= \tfrac{1}{2} \times 1000 \times 0.8 \times 15^2 \times 0.4$$
$$= 36\,000N$$

Drag is determined for the above section using the same formula, except for the use of a coefficient of drag. It is to be emphasized that the coefficient of drag is based upon the planform area when dealing with foils, and not cross-sectional area as is the case for obstructive forms. For this foil at an angle of attack of 3 degrees, the coefficient of drag could be 0.02 and so the drag:

$$F_D = \frac{1}{2} \times \rho \times a \times v^2 \times C_D$$
$$= \frac{1}{2} \times 1000 \times 0.8 \times 15^2 \times 0.02$$
$$= 1800N$$

The lift produced is fairly massive (over three and a half tons) and would be the kind of figure with which designers of small hydrofoil craft are familiar. Moreover, drag is a very reasonable 1800N (405lb) the *lift-drag ratio* of twenty demonstrating its efficiency. Lift-drag ratio does highlight the efficiency of a foil which, having flow on both surfaces, is about six times more efficient than a planing surface.

SUMMARY — LIFT PRODUCED BY AEROFOILS AND HYDROFOILS

1   Data resulting from model testing can be used to predict lift. The lift produced by a foil is given by $F_L = \frac{1}{2} \times \rho \times a \times v^2 \times C_L$ where the coefficient of lift is based upon the planform area. For compatibility, drag also is based upon the planform area.

2   As indicated by the force distribution, the centre of force of a foil, operating efficiently, is about 25 per cent aft of the leading edge, depending upon the foil's section and angle of attack.

3   At small angles of attack, high aspect ratio is beneficial to lift and lift-drag ratio, the latter giving an indication of efficiency.

Chapter 3

About Hull Design

Decisions, Decisions

A major difficulty facing the designer is that there are few absolutes. A design feature very suitable in one circumstance or weather condition may be a disaster in another. The designer must then decide whether there is an acceptable trade-off. Decisions, decisions.

An example is that of whether to design a boat as lightweight as it is possible to build it. Heavy displacement boats (displacement rela-ting to the water displaced by the hull and to the boat's weight) produce large wave systems and large wakes symbolic of high resistance. Very approximately, resistance varies directly with displacement (*see* Fig 39), and so if we increase displacement by 10 per cent, resistance goes up by the same amount at the same speed. Heavy displacement yachts are limited in their maximum speed because of their full-bodied hull form, while light displacement edges up the achievable top speed.

Fig 39   Obvious disturbance of the water by a displacement yacht.

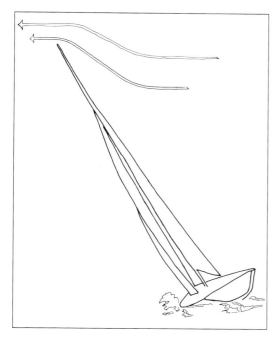

Fig 40   The sail's effectiveness is reduced by heeling.

It seems, then, that the direction to take is towards light displacement. Surely we must follow the dictum of Uffa Fox, that weight belongs only on steamrollers? Certainly steamrollers are hard to get going and to keep going, but they also are very hard to push over. Similarly, heavy displacement boats are more stable than light displacement boats. Taken to its extreme, a boat of no displacement in water (perhaps having a hull filled with helium) would have virtually no stability.

Low stability has a performance-sapping effect on sailing craft since they then have insufficient *power to carry sail*, that is, they will heel too readily in the wind. This reduces the sails' driving force, either because the wind tends to blow over the top of the sail (*see* Fig 40) or because it becomes necessary to reef in relatively light winds.

The problem of low stability for light displacement craft can be overcome by using large beam. But just when you thought it was safe to make a decision, it turns out that large beam introduces other problems. Water has little taste for going around large beams, and it retaliates by increasing hull drag. A secondary problem arises for beamy sailing craft when they heel in that the hull becomes unbalanced and difficult to keep on course.

An alternative way of incorporating large beam is by splitting the displacement between two hulls. Catamarans (and trimarans which actually spend their lives on two hulls) have the major advantage that each hull is much finer than that of a monohull, which means that the wave system it produces is small, and this removes the restraint on speed. The decision about displacement for multihulls is an easy one. Multihulls benefit from light displacement, adequate stability being obtained by beam as for monohulls. But fears about multihulls and beamy light displacement monohulls turning turtle and not recovering keep designers awake at night.

SUMMARY — DECISIONS, DECISIONS

1   A principal responsibility for the designer lies in making acceptable decisions. It can happen that a feature suitable for one circumstance or weather condition is totally unsuited to another.

2   A classic dilemma relates to displacement. Light displacement offers better high-speed performance but a lower level of stability not altogether satisfactorily compensated for by beam.

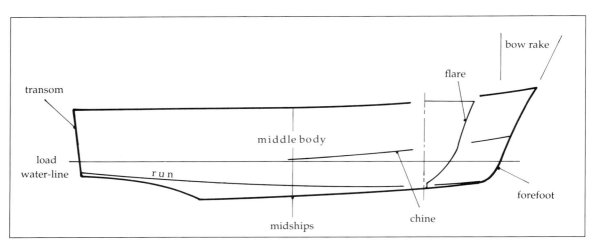

Fig 41   Terminology.

The Effect of the Driving Force

A walk around a harbour or marina reveals a wide variety of hull forms. Certain boat types are characterized by particular features (*see* Fig 41 for terminology). For example, sailing yachts often have raked bows, are fairly deep amidships, and usually have a fairly steep run aft to a transom which is out of the water. Sailing dinghies are usually much shallower and flatter in the bottom with a fairly level run aft. The run of fishing boats usually is less steep than for heavy displacement sailing yachts and leads to a deeply immersed transom. The bow usually has little rake, the forefoot is well immersed and the hull is deep and full bodied. This hull form contrasts vividly with the high-speed motor cruiser or power boat which has a steeply raked bow with little forefoot, a deep V-chined hull and a straight level run (*see* Figs 42–47).

It would be incorrect to suppose that each type has reached its pinnacle of design, otherwise there would be universality of form for each type. But while there might be similarity of, for example, fishing boats within a fleet in

Fig 42   The deep, immersed transom of a motor cruiser with planing performance.

Fig 43   A contrast of sterns for displacement craft – power and sail.

Fig 44   The flat bottom and straight run of a sailing dinghy.

Fig 45   In comparison, the displacement racing yacht has more V-shaped sections.

Fig 46   Earlier racing yachts tend to be deeper amidships.

Fig 47 A cruiser stern on a powered craft.

one country, elsewhere the hull form might be different, despite similar environmental conditions and fishing methods. Even though a fishing boat is functional above all else, fishermen do have beliefs about aspects of the hull form, such as the height or flare of the bows, and this influences designers and manufacturers who ultimately are market oriented.

However, these differences in form are not likely to be major because the fundamental requirements persist. Fishing boats are built like Chieftain tanks and carry a mountain of fish, which means that the displacement is high. Hence the hull form is full bodied. Similarly, a seagoing yacht's form is full bodied because it, too, has a high displacement. This comes largely from the heavy lead or cast-iron ballast keel that dangles under the hull so that it does not fall over when the wind fills the sails. Although the displacements of

both fishing boat and sailing yacht are high, the shape of the ends is very different. This is not the result of the designers pandering to the differing whims of fishermen and yachtsmen.

The effect of the driving force, either sail or propeller, has a significant bearing on hull form. The sailing yacht is being pushed along at a considerable height above the deck by the wind in the sails. This force at this position tends to bury the bow and lift the stern out of the water (*see* Figs 48a and 48b). If this tendency is not limited, the yacht may be driven under or at least there will be a loss of control, in particular a proneness to broaching in which the craft tends to round up towards the wind. Sailing in a combination of strong following wind and steep waves produces the likely conditions for bow burying to occur.

Bow burying is a singularly unpleasant experience – it has happened to me on both

Fig 48a   The yacht model exhibits bow up trim when towed at deck level.

Fig 48b   When allowance is made for the position of the sail driving force (by moving a weight forward on the deck) the model assumes a more level trim.

Fig 49a   A free sailing model before . . .

Fig 49b   . . . and after.

yachts and dinghies. One of these occasions was with a single-handed dinghy, the bow of which disappeared beneath the waves, quickly followed by the rest of the hull, leaving me swimming behind. Due to the buoyancy in the hull, it then popped out of the water backwards, breaking the mast in the process due to the extreme force of the wind in the sail. No sailing tactic other than reefing or sitting well aft can prevent this occurrence.

But there are design tactics which can be used. Increasing buoyancy forward is one approach, but the way this is accomplished is important. Designing the bow for greater fullness in the plan view of the hull may not be the most effective way. This lesson has been learned with dinghy catamarans where it has been found that such fullness produces high resistance as the bow, usually of only the leeward hull, starts to bury. As a result, there is a likelihood of the catamaran's tripping over this bow (*see* Figs 49a and 49b). A better solution is to increase freeboard forward while maintaining fineness (*see* Fig 50).

Fig 50   A catamaran's bow having adequate buoyancy with low resistance.

Another ploy is that of designing the bow so that the water produces a significant upward force as it flows past. If the water is directed downwards upon meeting the bow, the reaction will be upwards. Also, Bernoulli's theorem indicates that the force increases with the square of velocity and so a small increase in speed produces a relatively large improvement in resistance to bow burying. All this can be achieved by giving the bow rake, as seen in profile, because automatically this produces flare in the forward sections which turns the water downwards. The effectiveness of knuckles is offset by the drag they produce, and when bow burying occurs their angle of attack is reduced, thus lessening lift (*see* Figs 51 and 52).

A number of racing classes have zero bow rake, often as a result of class rules which impose few limitations, one of which is on overall length. Speed benefits by maximizing the length of the boat in contact with the water, and hence a vertical stem has become a common design feature among such classes. Although some flare can be built in to the bow, other approaches deserve examination.

Some years ago I produced a radical design to the International Offshore Rule, which comprises a complex of formulae, based on measurements of the design, aimed at assessing its performance. This particular design sought to take advantage of the way in which sailing length was assessed by utilizing an extremely low bow which would cut through minor waves rather than riding over them. The design looked destined for the sea bottom.

However, the testing of the model in the test tank, with appropriate allowance made for the position of the sail force, revealed a positive bow up trim with increasing speed (*see* Fig 53). This was achieved by designing the run so

Fig 51 A knuckle used on a large catamaran. If it should trip right over, the crew still can get out of the escape hatch.

Fig 52   A hull highly resistant to bow burying.

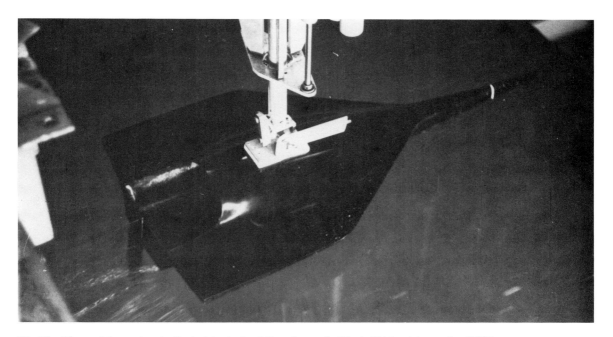

Fig 53   The model running in the test tank at a full scale speed of 7m/s (14 knots) on a 9m (30ft)
hull. At still higher speeds the bow trims up.

Fig 54   The low position of the propeller tends to cause bow up trim.

that it was steeper than typical for a light displacement hull. As the water flows aft, low pressure is created in this region which produces a downward force on the stern with, it has to be said, some increase in drag. A level run therefore would not be effective in preventing bow burying.

The raked, flared bow and steep run of the heavy displacement sailing yacht is justified. But this form would not be successful for a fishing boat or any powered craft for that matter. Since the propulsive force is below the water-line, the result would be an inordinate amount of bow up trim (*see* Fig 54).

For high-speed powered craft, the deep middle body would produce a downward

---

SUMMARY — THE EFFECT OF THE DRIVING FORCE

1   Whether a boat is driven by sail or propeller affects the hull form, a sail force tending to depress the bow and an engine's propulsion to raise the bow when these forces are high.

2   Bow burying, for sailing craft particularly, is avoided by a bow design which deflects the water downwards and which carries reserve buoyancy, but which does not lead to excessive resistance when the bow is depressed. A steep run creates a downward force aft which also assists.

3   Powered and planing craft generally require a large, buoyant stern with a moderate, shallow and level run depending upon expected speed.

force when the requirement for planing is that the hull is lifted partially from the water by its motion through the water. Thus some planing sailing dinghies are designed rather like power craft in the hope that the crew can sit far enough aft to avoid the funereal experience of bow burying. So the message must be 'bring out your bows'.

Wave Systems Created by Displacement Hulls

Boats described as being of *displacement* type are those which do not plane, essentially, even when a large amount of propulsive power is applied. The nature of the wave system generated around the hull is the stranglehold which inhibits planing and is an important factor affecting the performance of displacement craft.

Transverse waves, which are formed perpendicularly to the boat's centreline, are significant because, effectively, they move with the hull. *Divergent waves* leave the hull at a consistent angle and are not thought to have an effect once they have been generated (*see* Fig 55).

Because it is affected by the hull form and the interaction of the waves generated by the hull, the transverse wave system is complex. The bow wave is fundamental to the wave system. In Bernoullian tradition, the slowing of the water towards the bow produces a switch of energies. As there is a free surface, the water piles up to form a bow wave, the crest of which is formed a short distance aft of the forward end of the water-line (*see* Fig 56).

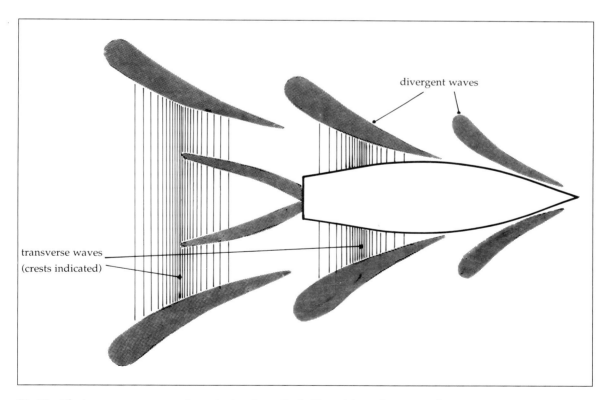

divergent waves

transverse waves
(crests indicated)

Fig 55   The transverse waves are important as far as the hull's resistance is concerned.

Fig 56   Swans have wave systems, too.

Interesting things now start to happen. The bow wave generates a wave system just as does a pebble dropped into water. For such a wave there is a relationship between its distance between crests, that is its *wavelength* (symbolized by the Greek letter lambda, λ), and velocity, and this takes the form:

$$\lambda = \frac{2 \times \pi \times V^2}{g}$$

Since the acceleration due to gravity g is 9.81m/s^2, the wavelength can be written as:

$$\lambda = 0.64 \times V^2$$

The boat can be thought to be travelling at the same speed as the wave is propagated because the boat and wave stay in the same relative position. Therefore, we can think of V as the velocity of the boat.

For example, if the boat's velocity is 3m/s (5.82 knots), the wavelength of the boat's transverse wave system would be:

$$\lambda = 0.64 \times 3^2 = 5.8\text{m} \; (\textit{see} \text{ Fig 57}).$$

Think of the boat moving through still water, unaffected by external waves. It is important to note that the boat's length or form makes no difference to the length of this wave, but its amplitude and shape are modified.

Aft of the middle body, as the hull narrows and the run steepens, there is a tendency to produce a hollow, and this is the beginning of the stern wave system. Although of smaller amplitude than the bow wave system, its length is the same. The overall wave system is the result of both bow and stern wave systems which interact according to the hull's speed.

At certain speeds, the wave systems will

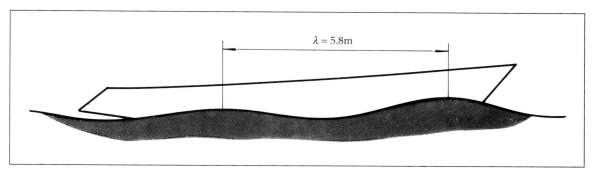

Fig 57   Wavelength is determined by velocity, and not the hull's length.

coincide, producing exaggerated crests and troughs. At other speeds, cancellation will occur, resulting in a lowered stern wave system (*see* Fig 58). The smaller the wave system, the less the energy required to produce it, and this is reflected in the resistance of the hull. The resistance is not affected as much as it may seem, except at higher speeds. At lower speeds, the wave system is of low significance and can be hard to distinguish towards the stern (*see* Figs 59 a–f).

When the wavelength approaches the length water-line, the first trough of the bow wave system starts to reinforce the initial hollow of the stern wave system. The stern squats in this large dent in the water, giving the hull an attitude problem. The trim increases as the speed increases, as if the boat is trying to climb its own bow wave, and can be likened to antisurfing (*see* Fig 60).

The speed at which this occurs is called the *maximum displacement speed* because the boat can go no faster in the displacement mode. It would not be correct to say that the displacement

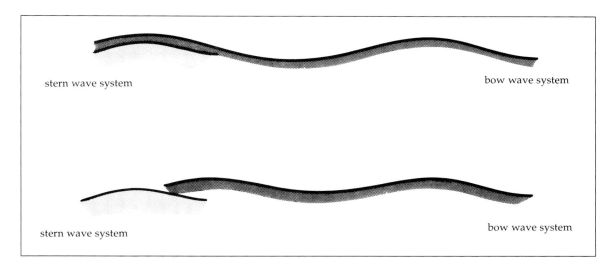

Fig 58   The separate bow and stern wave systems.

Figs 59(a–f)   This series shows the wave system of the model at increasing speed.

Fig 59(a)

Fig 59(b)

Fig 59(c)

Fig 59(d)

Fig 59(e)

Fig 59(f)

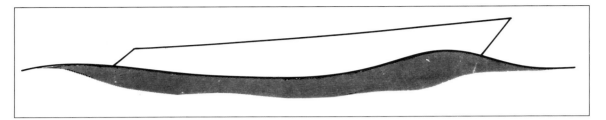

Fig 60   The hull effectively is being pushed uphill.

hull cannot exceed this speed, but rather that it is unsuited to it. This was emphasized to me when once, faced with a flat calm and no engine, I begged a tow from the skipper of an MFV (motor fishing vessel) called Alf (the skipper, not the vessel). Alf knew all about people begging from him, evidenced by the liquid payment he extracted from me, and he knew all about towing, judging by the hawser which was as thick as a docker's arm.

What he didn't seem to know about was towing small sailing cruisers, and I am certain he knew absolutely nothing of wave systems. When the hawser was tied in place and we were both satisfied, he stepped into his wheel-house and did not look back. He throttled up to eight or nine knots (4–4½m/s) and the hawser stretched visibly. My small cruiser's stern sank into the trough it created, the crest of the wave system's second wave making a mess of the sea some distance behind. The amount by which the bow trimmed up was such that frantic waving for Alf to slow down could not be seen, even had he been looking.

Alf's world on the MFV was a relatively peaceful one. He was cruising along, not hard-pressed, quite below his pride and joy's max-imum displacement speed. With a water-line length of around 18m, the wave system could reasonably be extended a little beyond this to perhaps 19m, at which point he would be at maximum displacement speed. Using the for-mula presented, the speed is calculated to be 5.4m/s (10.6 knots) for λ = 19m.

Meanwhile, I had to grit my teeth and hope the foredeck cleat could stand the load and that my boat could stand the excitement of travelling at one and half times the maximum speed she was meant to.

The maximum wavelength a displacement craft can produce reasonably is referred to as its *displaced length*, this being about 19m for Alf's MFV. For my small cruiser of 6.7m length overall and 5.5m length water-line, its displaced length probably would have been about 6.2m, signifying a maximum displace-ment speed of 3.1m/s (6.0 knots). Thus, big'uns are faster than little'uns (*see* Fig 61).

A means of gauging a boat's speed, taking account of its length, is by using *Froude num-ber*, named after William Froude and sym-bolized by *Fr* (or *Fn*). Froude number does for hulls on the water surface what Reynolds number does for fully submerged bodies. Both measure speed with length as a criterion, but the former relates to waves and the latter to flow conditions.

The principle is that two craft have the same Froude number if the length of the wave sys-tem relative to water-line length is the same. Froude number is defined by:

$$Fr = \frac{V}{\sqrt{g \times LWL}}$$

where *V* is velocity of the boat, and *LWL* is the length water-line. For example, Alf's MFV at 4.5m/s and length water-line of 18m would

Fig 61   Converting a little'un to a big'un by extending the stern has little effect on resistance in this case because, although water is in contact with the extension, little water is displaced by it and therefore the displaced length is barely increased.

indicate a Froude number of 0.34, while my small cruiser at the same speed and of length water-line 5.5m would have been towed at a Froude number of 0.61.

The typical Froude number representing maximum displacement speed is about 0.40, but this varies with hull form. For instance, an older-style yacht having long overhangs with the capability of extending its wave system well beyond its water-line endings, would achieve a higher Froude number than this. For a general assessment of maximum displacement speed 0.40 is a fair average.

A length water-line of 10m indicates a maximum displacement speed of 4.0m/s (7.7 knots) and an eighteenth-century clipper ship of water-line length 69m a maximum speed of

10.4m/s (20.2 knots). Since a record average passage speed of eighteen knots has been recorded for a clipper ship, it therefore must have been sailing at or close to its maximum displacement speed for much of the time.

The Distribution of Displacement for Sailing Craft

The quest for good performance starts with the shape of the hull, particularly below the water-line. It generally pays to maximize displaced length within the constraint of the length water-line or length overall, enabling a higher speed to be reached. Displaced length

SUMMARY — WAVE SYSTEMS CREATED BY DISPLACEMENT HULLS

1 As it moves through the water, a boat's hull produces both a transverse and a divergent wave system, although only the former appears to affect the resistance of the hull.

2 The transverse wave system results from the interaction of the bow and stern wave systems, and varies with the boat's velocity. At maximum displacement speed, the hollow of the stern wave is reinforced, causing the boat to trim up at the bow, a state which carries high resistance.

3 A boat's velocity with reference to its wave system and length water-line is judged by Froude number:

$$Fr = \frac{V}{\sqrt{g \times LWL}}$$

Maximum displacement speed is indicated by a Froude number of about 0.4, depending upon the hull's displaced length.

is enhanced by the hull's capability of generating a longer wave system by a bow wave which forms earlier and a stern wave which extends as far aft as possible.

Overhang at the bow causes the bow wave to creep forward, and because of the sectional form usually produced by overhang (*see* Fig 62), the displaced length is increased substantially when heeling. A full bow generates an earlier wave, though the same effect would result from a deep forefoot which retains reasonably fine water-lines forward (*see* Fig 63). In general, this is achieved by an increase in volume of displacement forward. If taken to any kind of extreme, however, additional drag would result owing to the size of the bow wave formed – a problem encountered especially by full bows.

An intriguing approach to achieving a bow wave shift, whilst at the same time bringing about a possible reduction in the height of the bow wave, lies in the use of the bulbous bow (*see* Fig 64). We can think of the bow producing one system and the bulb another, the interaction, one theory suggests, resulting in an out of phase cancellation effect (*see* Figs 65–6).

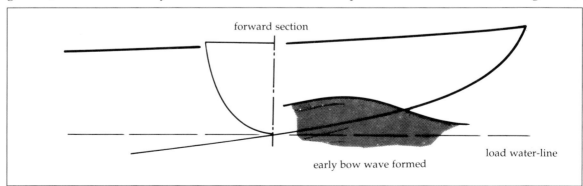

Fig 62 Long bow overhang.

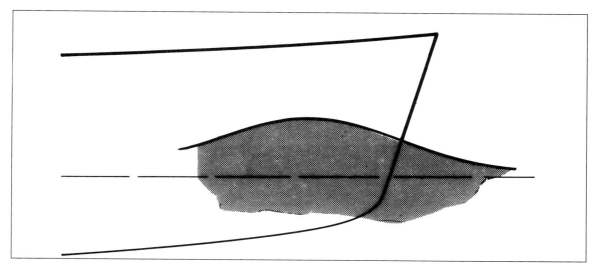

Fig 63   Displaced length is improved by a deep forefoot, but behaviour in following seas may be compromised.

Fig 64   A bulbous bow on a sailing yacht. It is likely to be more effective in flat water than in a seaway.

Increasing the fullness at the stern is similarly effective. The complexity of the stern wave system, whose pattern and interactions with the bow wave system alter with speed, militates against the use of a bulb which at the stern would tend to be suited to one speed only. However, consideration can be given to

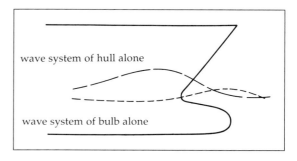

wave system of hull alone

wave system of bulb alone

Fig 65   The theoretical independent wave systems of the hull alone and the bulbous bow. It has been supposed that the two interact producing a final, diminished wave, though one series of tests has indicated that the two cannot be superimposed in this way.

Fig 66a and b   There is little evidence of a diminution of the bow wave for the model with the bulbous bow compared to the one without. The bulbous bow does decrease resistance slightly in some conditions because of the improvement in displaced length.

Fig 67   An example of a bustle.

design of the aft end at or around maximum displacement speed.

Bustles (*see* Fig 67) have been used on sailing yachts to increase the volume of displacement towards the aft end of the water-line, to delay separation and to reduce the resistance caused by the wave system. But drag from the resulting wake can be higher than for the hull without the bustle. Generally, it is felt that the aft end should not take up an angle to the ambient water flow greater than about 13–15 degrees if *separation*, in which the water flow tends to reverse, is to be kept to a minimum. For high displacement speeds, then, the hull form needs to be designed with its volume of displacement somewhat shifted from the middle body to the ends, provided the bow is not too obstructive (i.e. blunt) and an excessive wake is not produced aft.

One criterion used to assess the distribution of displacement is *prismatic coefficient*, which is the ratio of the volume of displacement to the volume of a particular prism which surrounds it. This prism is formed by the length water-line and the *section* having the largest area up to the water-line, usually just aft of the middle of the boat. (A section is an imaginary vertical and transverse plane (*see* Fig 68).) For example, if the volume of displacement is 3m³ and the volume of the prism is 6m³, then the prismatic coefficient is 3:6, usually expressed as 0.5. Experimentation indicates that prismatic coefficient should be around or above 0.6 for a sailing yacht to perform with least resistance at a Froude number of 0.4.

At lower speeds, when displaced length is not an issue, the ideal hull form will be finer at the ends, particularly at the stern. Because wave-making is less significant, the hull can be designed more closely to the kind of shape used for totally submerged bodies, that is with rather full middle body and fine tapering

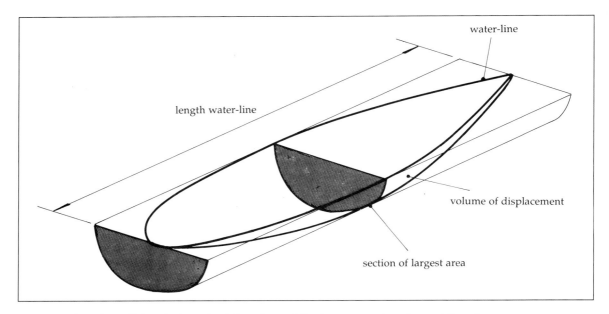

Fig 68   Prismatic coefficient is the ratio of the volume of displacement to the volume of the prism.

stern. Again from experiment, a prismatic co-efficient of about 0.53 has been found suitable for a sailing yacht at a Froude number of 0.2–0.3.

These figures represent guidelines only in order to emphasize the principles, simply because much depends upon the way the experimental hull forms were modified to obtain higher or lower prismatic coefficients. A yacht having a high prismatic coefficient will be slightly slower in light winds than a yacht of low prismatic coefficient form, and vice versa.

In some conflict is the requirement for a reasonably fine entry at higher speeds. It is generally felt that the *half angle of entrance*, which is defined by the angle between the water-line and the centreline in plan (*see* Fig 69), should be about 10 degrees for efficiency at maximum displacement speeds. Lower speeds favour a larger half angle (up to 30 degrees at very low speeds) when wave-making is small and the yacht can more closely resemble the streamlined underwater form.

Higher speeds also benefit from a fuller stern, particularly of the transom type (*see* Fig 70).

These factors can be described by the *longitudinal centre of buoyancy*, which is the longitudinal centre of gravity or balance point of the displaced water (think of it as a block of ice). Often the longitudinal centre of buoyancy is expressed as a percentage of the water-line

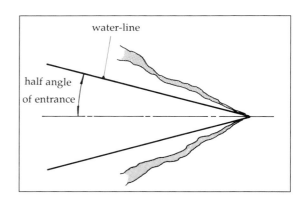

Fig 69   Half angle of entrance.

Fig 70   Transom-type sterns are of benefit at higher speeds, especially sailing downwind when surfing on waves is possible.

length aft of the forward ending of the water-line. Again, 'best' figures have been suggested from experiments of yacht hulls at around 49 per cent for slow speeds, 51 per cent at a Froude number of 0.3 and as much as 56 per cent at a Froude number at or above 0.4.

Therefore, likely sailing speed, resulting from the most common wind speeds likely to be encountered, defines the requirement both for prismatic coefficient and for longitudinal centre of buoyancy. This presents yet another Difficult Design Decision.

SUMMARY — THE DISTRIBUTION OF DISPLACEMENT FOR SAILING CRAFT

1   A boat's maximum displacement speed is high when the hull can produce an extended wave system, achieved by distributing the displacement away from the middle body and towards the ends. For least resistance at a Froude number at or above 0.4, prismatic coefficient for yachts should be about 0.6 or more.

2   For performance at higher velocities, the half angle of entrance should be as little as 10 degrees and a full, perhaps transom type of stern used. The longitudinal centre of buoyancy should be about 56 per cent at a Froude number at or above 0.4.

3   At a low Froude number, resistance is least when the prismatic coefficient is low and the longitudinal centre of buoyancy is positioned at about amidships, in which case the hull form is similar to a streamlined, totally immersed body.

The Pitching of Sailing Craft

A friend, with a good deal of experience with boats and boat building, once was testing a model and declared that it performed better backwards than forwards. This, I hasten to add, resulted from an accident during his test procedure. Testers of models regard this as a Serious Business, and resent any inference of playing with toys.

This serendipity has influenced his thinking, though I cannot say it has mine. If we reshape our bows so that they are full and buxom, and our sterns so that they are fine, we just might find some advantage at low speeds when sailing with the wind. Sailing to windward into waves, this hull form would be abominable.

Even discounting the effect of a flat transom occasionally hitting the seas, the drawback is that every time a wave meets the bow, the shape and buoyancy of the forward sections lift the bow rapidly. This initiates *pitching*, which describes that awful hobby-horse motion guaranteed to reproduce the foredeck hand's breakfast.

But the real disadvantage is that pitching is most detrimental to performance. Once pitching is initiated it tends to persist if the wave frequency coincides with the boat's rhythm.

The movement at the top of the mast is extreme. As the bow plunges, the wind draws ahead and as the bow rises, the wind blows from the beam. As a consequence, the sails alternately flap and are stalled, neither state being efficient. The drive from the sails is reduced substantially (*see* Fig 71).

Pitching is a form of harmonic motion which is minimized by ensuring that the excitation response is low. This is achieved by a bow designed with low volume, particularly above the water-line, and with a gradual take-up of buoyancy so that the bow is not accelerated sharply upwards. Flare and bow overhang therefore are ill advised. The yacht's heeling complicates the problem further because a V-shaped section produces high acceleration. A U-shaped section is a better solution (*see* Fig 72).

The stern shape also plays an important part. As the bow rises, so the stern plunges and if it takes up buoyancy quickly it will damp the pitching sequence (think of a pendulum in water). The type of stern suitable is therefore completely opposite in form to that of the bow. That is to say, we desire a wide flat stern of long low overhang (*see* Fig 73).

It may have been spotted that the bow and stern shapes advocated for a low-pitch hull form are in complete contradiction to those suggested to eliminate bow burying. The anti-

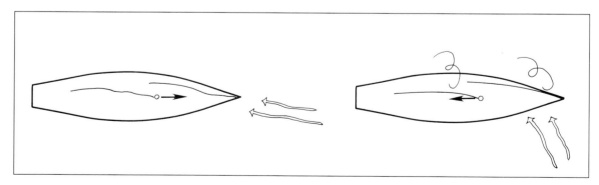

Fig 71   As the boat pitches, the wind alternately draws ahead and then frees.

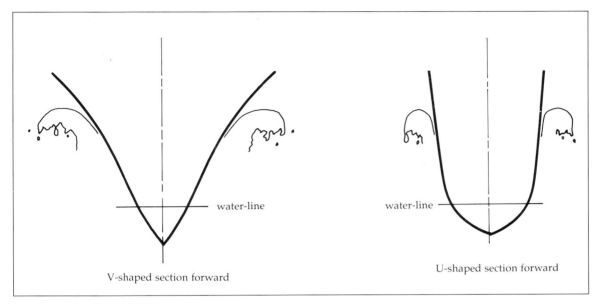

water-line

V-shaped section forward

water-line

U-shaped section forward

Fig 72   Particularly when heeled, the fine U-shaped section is favoured in a seaway.

pitching lobby may have a loud voice for the racers, and the anti-bow-burying lobby may speak for the cruisers. Of course, a boat which bow buries may not even come last; the saying that 'to finish first, first you must finish' springs to mind.

I have avoided suggesting that what is sought is a much loved 'compromise' because this always seems to produce solutions exactly half-way between the extremes. A variety of factors affects bow and stern shapes and it could be right to adopt an extreme. Responsibility cannot be abrogated under the guise of compromise, which means that the designer is stuck with yet another Difficult Design Decision.

Another factor which influences pitching is the disposition of mass on board. There is a paranoia about concentrating mass amidships and so builders of racing yachts and dinghies

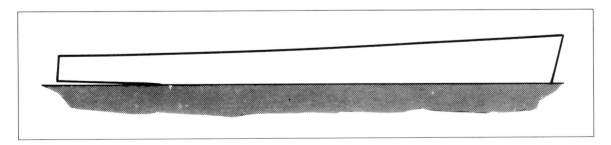

Fig 73   A bow of short overhang produces minimal pitch excitation, and the long low overhang of the stern damps pitching.

pare down the hull weight in the bows and stern; sails and other equipment are located in the middle of yachts (but only where this is legal within racing rules, of course) and the helmsman and crew of sailing dinghies cuddle up together.

The theory underpinning all these strange practices is that the boat should make a habit of losing its pitching momentum quickly. A see-saw, analogously, is much easier to stop when people sit close to the middle rather than at the ends. The effect of distance is, in fact, a squared function, and so mass a short distance from the centre of gravity has a small effect while mass at a large distance has considerable effect.

It can be seen that mass in a ballast keel is significant, being some distance from the centre of gravity, though vertically in this case. There have been examples of designs where the ballast at the bottom of the keel has been kept to a minimum in order to minimize this pendulum effect, but there are other factors which affect the issue. Because of the distance of the masthead from the centre of gravity, mass here will be very influential, and indeed from this point of view the mast should be as lightweight as possible.

Like many theories, the value of concentrating masses is difficult to prove. It could be hypothesized that a boat light in the ends responds too readily to the waves, thus exciting pitching. It could also be argued that a mis-

match of the boat's pitch frequency and the waves' periodicity is the real target. Nevertheless, mass concentration does appear to aid performance.

Planing Craft Design

Although it would be supercilious to suggest that planing craft are no more than flat plates which are adapted, it is true that the flat surface has provided the basis for much research. In this form, analysis is reasonably straightforward and, from this point, allowances can be made for variations in the curvature or angles of the bottom.

At speed, a planing craft's weight is supported primarily by the lift force generated by the water being deflected downwards by the hull bottom. The high pressure, and hence force, on the bottom resulting from this deflection is not uniform but is at its highest close to where the water first meets the hull, this point being termed the *spray root*. Fig 74 indicates a typical force distribution for a flat plate. Using Bernoulli's theorem, the actual forces of lift and drag can be calculated. This is not so easy (in fact, it is difficult) for displacement craft because of the wave system, which complicates matters.

Take the flat plate to sea, keep it planing, and it really does not miss having topsides or a transom. Buoyancy is not needed when all

---

SUMMARY — THE PITCHING OF SAILING CRAFT

1   The pitching of a sailing craft is detrimental to performance principally because of the reduction in efficiency of the sails.

2   Fine U-shaped bows of short overhang produce least pitch excitation, and full sterns having long, low overhang most effectively damp pitching.

3   Masses concentrated around the middle of the boat, in both the longitudinal and vertical senses, appear to aid a sailing craft's pitch response in waves.

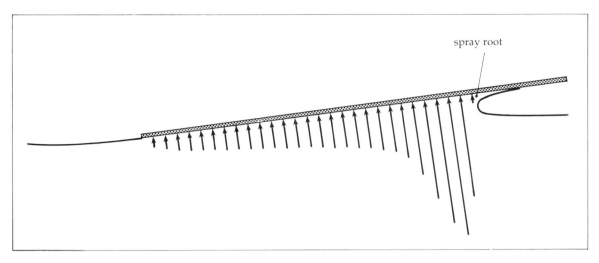

Fig 74   Force distribution on a planing flat plate.

lift is produced by forward motion. Occasionally, though, waves come over the front and it looks as if it would be better to curve up the front like a ski. The other drawback is that it tends to loosen the fillings in your teeth from continually slamming into the waves.

Powered planing craft need to be more seaworthy than this, not only from the point of view of the crew's comfort, but also in order for the hull to hang together. Seaworthiness is achieved, notably, by incorporating *deadrise* in the hull. We can imagine bending the plate along the centreline and lifting the two edges (*see* Fig 75). The angle which each half makes with the horizontal is termed, rather obviously, the *angle of deadrise* (*see* Fig 76).

There is a price to pay for deadrise. As the hull cleaves the water, making for an easier entry, the water tends to travel outwards and therefore is not deflected downwards so effectively. The consequence is a loss in efficiency which ultimately leads to higher hull resistance. In order to produce sufficient lift to support the boat, the hull of high deadrise runs at a greater angle of bow up trim. Very high-speed power boats, with angles of deadrise

close to 25 degrees, run at around an optimum 8-degree trim, compared with 4 degrees for a flat planing surface. This extreme trim, together with the loss of lift resulting from deep V hull forms, limits deadrise effectively to around 28 degrees.

Fig 75   Deadrise.

Fig 76   *An angle of deadrise of 22 degrees.*

Deep V hulls give good seakeeping, a softer ride and an ability to stay on course easily, known as *directional stability*. But at low velocities this hull form produces low lift and must trim up to an extreme to overcome the severe increase in resistance at maximum displacement speed (often referred to as *hump speed* as a description of the shape of this section of the resistance against velocity curve (*see* Fig 77)).

Perhaps because of the deep V's high-speed, race-bred, prop-riding image, powered craft of the motor cruiser type have been designed with similar deadrise angles. Probably this is a mistake because there would be a substantial reduction in resistance and hence

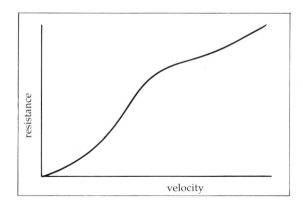

Fig 77   *Resistance against velocity curve. The 'hump' in the curve occurs at maximum speed in displacement mode.*

fuel consumption if a smaller deadrise angle were used. A reduction from 25 to 15 degrees gives an improvement in economy of up to 15 per cent, to borrow a phrase used by those selling economy devices for cars. A realistic reduction in fuel used is 10 per cent.

Hulls with shallower deadrise often are classified as semi V or moderate V. All three types discussed are usually of constant deadrise along the hull's length. Warped-bottomed power boats, in which the transom is near flat and the angle of deadrise increases forward, are rather old hat and tend to have the advantages and disadvantages diametrically opposed to the deep V form. One disadvantage to be highlighted is that warped bottoms tend to result in a hull which is overly sensitive, particularly to *heaving* in which the hull is lifted in response to relatively minor waves or changes in trim. A power boat which heaves readily is not at its best at sea (who is, indeed?!).

Powered craft which run wholly on dynamic lift tend to be prone to heaving and also to the aptly termed *porpoising*. There is no doubt that planing craft are better behaved if a proportion of the lift is from the buoyancy of the hull. Low-speed planing craft and semi-planing types become more friendly at sea by deliberately reducing the dynamic lift, achieved by using a round bilged form aft, or by slowing down. A deep, wide transom is still required in order to prevent the stern squatting.

Sailing dinghies which are sufficiently lightweight will usually plane even in light to moderate winds. Nevertheless, for a large proportion of their sailing time they perform as displacement craft and therefore the hull form needs to be adaptable for both modes. At the design stage it is best to err on the side of the planing form, that is by using a fairly straight run and large transom, because in light winds or when not planing the crew can

Fig 78   A sailing dinghy, essentially of planing form.

Fig 79   Flaps, sometimes called trim tabs, to adjust trim.

sit forward of their usual station to trim the boat and reduce transom drag (*see* Fig 78).

Control of trim for planing craft is achieved mainly by the design of the run, but, for powered craft, *transom flaps* provide an ancillary trim control. These flaps hinge on the bottom edge of the transom and, when lowered, reduce the bow up trim (*see* Fig 79). Trim also can be controlled if the drive system is free to articulate, in which case the propeller and prop shaft can be angled for the appropriate trim. The foremost system incorporating hydraulic power trim is the Arneson drive.

Another system of control of a sort is the use of a series of *spray rails* of triangular section running fore and aft (*see* Fig 80). When the power craft is heeled, the flow of water produces a stabilizing force (*see* Fig 81). Spray

Fig 80   Spray rails.

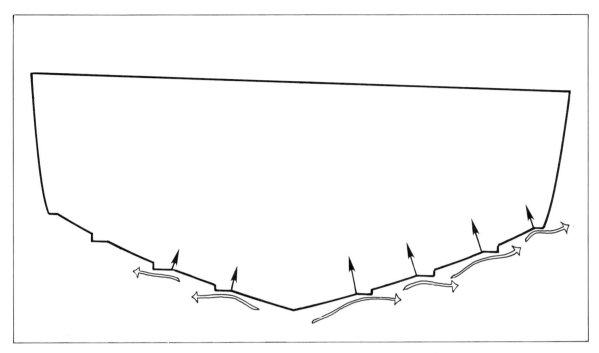

Fig 81   The flow of water produces forces tending to right the hull.

rails also prevent the water from remaining attached to the hull and this reduces the wetted contact, a significant resistance factor for planing craft.

The same principle applies to *stepped hulls* which are designed with one or more transverse steps in the hull. Ultra-high-speed racing craft, of the kind which outsprint Formula One racing cars and have a higher top speed than a typical hot hatchback, usually use stepped hulls, often of catamaran configuration so that they ride on four points. This reduces wetted area considerably and gives good stability, which is necessary at these speeds.

SUMMARY — PLANING CRAFT DESIGN

1   A craft planes when a substantial lift force results from the water impinging on the planing surface at speed. The force distribution indicates a large force close to the spray root.

2   Deadrise is incorporated into a planing hull so that it penetrates waves more easily and to ensure that there is some lift from the buoyancy of the hull, which lessens heave. Economy is affected adversely by deadrise (1 per cent per degree).

3   Transom flaps, spray rails and stepped hulls provide stability and satisfactory planing performance at speed.

Stability

The diverse conditions a hull encounters on the water, such as when travelling at high speed, moored up in harbour, or battling through the waves, generate quite different requirements for stability. All three relate to the boat's remaining deck uppermost and any deviation from this state we hope should result in a restoring tendency. Thus, we think of a boat as being stable if it returns to the normal when a force causing heel or trim is removed.

Achieving stability in very high-speed craft is perhaps the most difficult of the three. Often the balance of forces is so tenuous that it can easily be upset. For example, the combination of an over-enthusiastic throttle person and an awkward wave can throw a power boat in the air, and who knows how it will land. Once airborne, natural stability is lost except perhaps where deliberate aerodynamic stabilizing surfaces are built in. Even then, aircraft-like stability is not easy to achieve on a hull which adopts such a large variance of angle of attack.

Balance is maintained most easily where the lift surface is multipoint, and hydrofoil craft successfully use this principle. Otherwise, the best one can do is to ensure that the centre of gravity is located directly over the lift surface so that reasonable balance is maintained. It makes sense to design fast boats with a centre of gravity further aft to match the rear-ward shift of the centre of the lift force and centre of buoyancy. While a low centre of gravity benefits transverse stability, the dynamic lift forces of the water acting on the hull are more significant for high-speed craft.

The forces affecting displacement craft in waves are of the buoyant kind. A particular stability problem occurs with powered craft when in a following sea. At times the hull is supported by waves at bow and stern, which results in a severe reduction of transverse stability. If this is coupled with a raised centre of gravity, brought about for instance by a large load of fish which also can slither from side to side, it is not surprising that boats fall over at sea and don't get up. When the bow and stern are left clear of the water, only the middle part being supported, capsize is less likely because beam is so influential in providing transverse stability.

Just as beam works for transverse stability, length is an important factor in preventing *pitchpoling*, which is demonstrated by the boat's buttocks going over its elbow. Pitchpoling is relatively rare and goes hand in hand with the kind of conditions where experienced sailors speak of rogue waves, drogues, pouring oil on the water and manning the liferafts. It is usually felt that the canoe stern is favourite for these conditions since its shape is similar to that of the bow and thus the following, overtaking seas will be parted (*see* Fig 82).

In the midst of all this high-speed and high-storm excitement relating to *dynamical stability*, any interest in *statical stability* when bobbing about on the marina pontoon seems not only dull but somewhat ludicrous. But we do need to ensure that when the party is in full swing and all the merrymakers stagger to one side of *Gin Palace II* to watch Hooray Henry paddling in the water, they and *GP II* don't roll drunkenly into the drink. Knowing about transverse statical stability also helps us to calculate the power to carry sail for yachts, and provides an indicator of dynamical stability.

Initial transverse stability when in the upright position can be assessed by moving a weight across the boat a given distance and measuring how much heel this induces (*see* Fig 83). Using this criterion, we can see that a large ferry is more stable than a small yacht. But heel both craft through 90 degrees and the yacht is likely to right itself while the ferry capsizes, indicating that in this state the yacht has greater stability.

Fig 82   A canoe-sterned yacht.

Fig 83   An indication of stability is given by the crew christening their deck shoes.

Fig 84   Extended topsides and a high doghouse assist righting when inverted.

At large angles of heel, the factors which improve stability differ from those which are significant at small angles. The yacht benefits from having a deep ballast keel and this results in a low centre of gravity which can be thought of as levering the yacht upright. Another beneficial factor is a high coachroof which extends well outboard so that its buoyancy tends to right the yacht at extremes of heel (*see* Fig 84). Lifeboats take the principle further and some use an inflatable bag within the deck superstructure for guaranteed self-righting.

The relationship between the centres of buoyancy and gravity determines stability. Fig 85 shows the section of a vessel which is heeled as a result of either a shifted weight, ballast or people, or as a result of the wind force on the sail plan. The centre of buoyancy shifts outboard to a greater or lesser extent depending upon the beam and general hull form.

Although not an accurate way of describing it, the centre of buoyancy can be likened to a pivot point. The forces acting on the boat are very similar to those on a heeled armchair, which I present as a parallel for armchair sailors (*see* Fig 85). The armchair is seen to be stable at this angle of heel because its weight, acting at the centre of gravity, is to the right of the feet supporting the chair. It is to be noted that it is not a requirement for stability that the

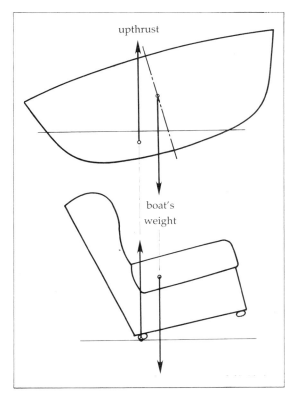

upthrust

boat's
weight

*Fig 85   Hulls are just like armchairs, which
armchair sailors have known all along.*

centre of gravity, either for armchair or boat,
is below either the feet or the centre of
buoyancy.

As the armchair is heeled further, a point is
reached at which the centre of gravity lies directly above the pivot, thus producing neutral
stability. Narrow, heavily ballasted yachts do
not reach neutral stability until virtually inverted, depending upon coachroof buoyancy.
Most craft experience a point of *vanishing
stability* when heeled. A *stability curve* is often
constructed at the design stage so that this
point can be established and to highlight the
angle of heel at which maximum stability
occurs (*see* Fig 86).

If, at a particular angle of heel, a line is

drawn vertically through the centre of buoyancy, it intersects the centreline at a point de-
noted by the *metacentre* (*see* Fig 87). Although
the position of the metacentre is unique to the
angle of heel, radical shifts of the metacentre
are unlikely within a 'normal' range of heel
angle. The position of the metacentre is fixed
only by the geometry of the hull, because of its
effect on the shift of buoyancy (except at extremes of heel when the coachroof plays a
part). Catamarans have very high metacentres
(*see* Fig 88).

Naval architecture is preoccupied with
metacentres, perhaps not unreasonably because ships live or die by their position relative to the centre of gravity. If you like
contemplating naval matters, think about
adding weight at the metacentre when the
boat or vessel is heeled. There should be no
change in heel. This does represent a method,
though not a recognized one, for finding the
position of the metacentre.

The distance between the metacentre and
the centre of gravity, termed the *metacentric
height*, provides a fundamental measure of
stability. A large value for the metacentric
height is a big step towards a high measure of
stability. The other factor of no small importance is the boat's weight (*see* Fig 89).

It seems that we should aim for as large a
metacentric height as possible. At times, the
price may be too high, in that excesses of ballast would be needed to lower the centre of
gravity, and weight is wasteful in terms of
performance. It is probably more sensible to
think in terms of the provision of an adequate
metacentric height. It is of interest that values
are little different for ships in comparison
with small craft.

A disadvantage of a large metacentric
height is that it can make for an uncomfortable
boat. The rolling period (the time taken to roll
to one side and back again) becomes faster as
metacentric height increases. Some sailing
yachts have uncomfortably quick motions.

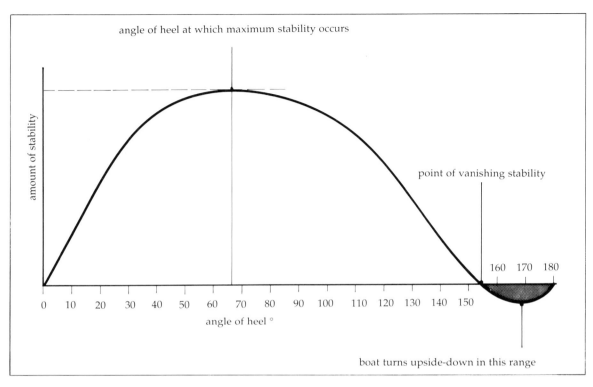

Fig 86   Stability at different angles of heel.

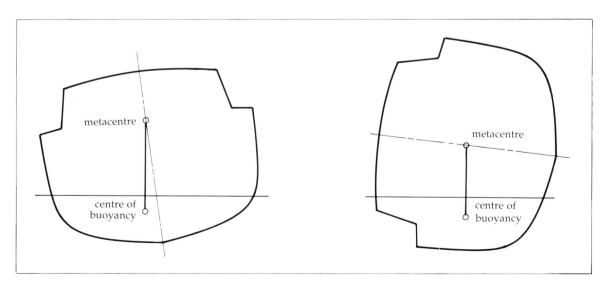

Fig 87   Establishing the metacentre.

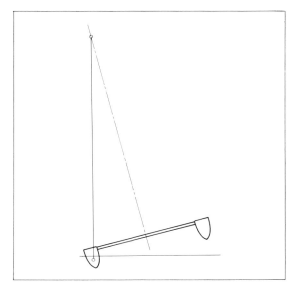

Fig 88   Catamarans usually have high metacentres.

Although comfort on board can be improved by providing heavily sprung armchairs for the crew, it makes more sense to deal with the origins of the motion. Underwater surfaces like keels damp this motion (that is to say, they reduce quickly the angle of roll, though do not change its period) and so a keel of large surface area is of benefit in this respect. Masses disposed vertically limit the initiation of rolling, and so a heavy mast, in particular, helps a great deal.

The reader may realize that this recommendation is completely opposite to the requirement for sailing to windward in waves, when a lightweight mast is regarded as a must. We can make a design decision (not a Difficult one) based upon whether the yacht is for cruising (use a heavyish mast) or for racing (use a lightweight mast).

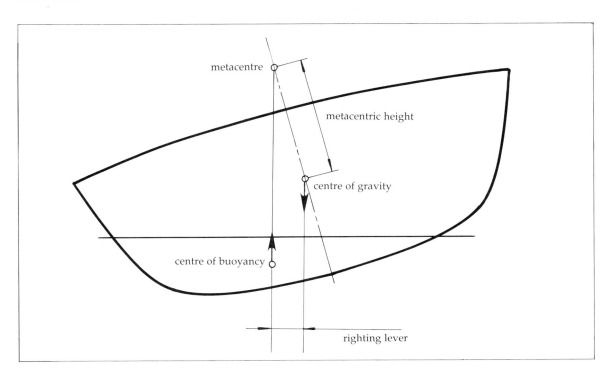

Fig 89   Stability is a product of the righting lever and the boat's weight.

SUMMARY — STABILITY

1   A vessel is defined as transversely stable at a particular angle of heel if it rights itself when the heeling tendency is removed.

2   Stability, both transversely and longitudinally, may be reduced in waves. Dynamic forces affect stability at high speeds.

3   Statical stability depends upon both the vessel's displacement and the metacentric height. The metacentric height is the distance between the centre of gravity and the metacentre (determined by the hull form). When the metacentric height reaches zero with increasing heel, the transverse stability curve indicates the point of vanishing stability.

4   A large metacentric height tends to result in a very quick motion which can be uncomfortable.

The Components of Resistance

When a boat travels through the water, there is a resistance caused which equates with the propulsive force from whatever source, the sails or propeller being two examples. It may seem surprising that the two are equal, that the propulsive force is not just a little greater than the resistance. It may help to think about a speedboat accelerated from a standstill by the outboard engine's propeller producing a force of, say, 1200N. When it reaches 3m/s, its resistance might be 250N. The resistive force is less than the propulsive force, so the speedboat continues to accelerate. At 7.1m/s resistance might be 1199N so it has just a little more to go. At 7.105m/s resistance might be 1200N and there is an exact match (*see* Fig 90).

Given the resistance (or propulsive force) and the boat's speed, the power requirement can be calculated. Power (in watts) is given by the product of resistance (in N) and speed (in m/s). Thus the power required from the propeller of the speedboat is $7.105 \times 1200 = 8526w$. Now, the propeller is not ultra-efficient and the losses it suffers plus those of the engine's transmission in total are in the order of 55 per cent. Therefore, 8526W must represent 45 per cent of the engine's delivered power, which therefore must be 18947W (which equals 25.4 horsepower). It follows that an outboard producing about 19kW would propel the speedboat at just over 7m/s.

A large proportion of the speedboat's resistance at this speed would be *induced resistance*, the by-product of the lift force fundamental to planing. Also significant would be *surface frictional resistance* produced as water flows past the surface. The outboard leg causes *appendage resistance* and the above-water hull, windscreen, people and outboard result in *air resistance*.

A significant part of the total resistance at lower sub-planing speeds would be *wave-making resistance* resulting from the production of waves, together with *viscous pressure resistance* which is the equivalent of form drag around a submerged body. *Eddy-making resistance*, resulting from eddies formed at the transom and from discontinuities such as spray rails, would also contribute.

Although not applicable to powered craft, *heeling resistance* is a factor for sailing craft. This is measured in terms of the additional resistance when heeled as opposed to upright. Similarly,

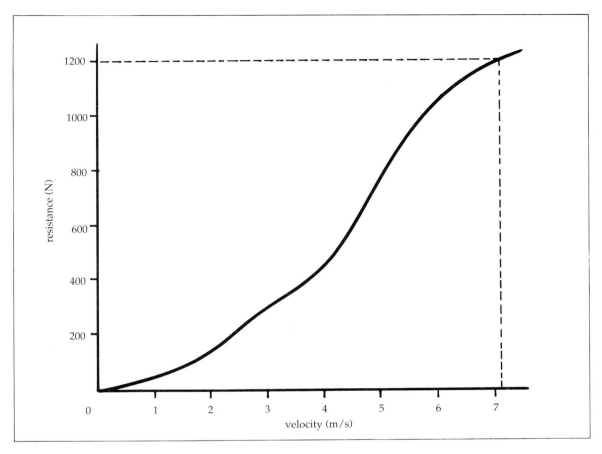

Fig 90   At 7.105m/s, resistance is 1200N.

induced resistance is an add-on from the base of zero trim or, for sailing craft, zero leeway.

Each is a component of the total resistance and the proportion of each varies according to the boat's type, its hull form and its speed (*see* Fig 91). For example, the principal resistance for a displacement craft when hard pressed is wave-making, but at low speed when the wave system developed is small, the most significant component is frictional resistance.

Frictional resistance is calculable fairly readily, Bernoulli's theorem providing a means of so doing. In this case, the frictional resistance is given by $R_F = \frac{1}{2} \times \rho \times a \times v^2 \times C_F$. The density of sea water ρ would be typically 1025kg/m³. The area a which is relevant is the wetted surface area measured in square metres. The velocity v is straightforward enough; its units are m/s. From the formula it is to be noted that frictional resistance increases as the square of velocity. (If we double the velocity, we quadruple the frictional resistance.)

The part of this formula which is not so straightforward is the *coefficient of friction*, C_F. This coefficient, like the coefficient of drag, provides a measure of efficiency and relates to

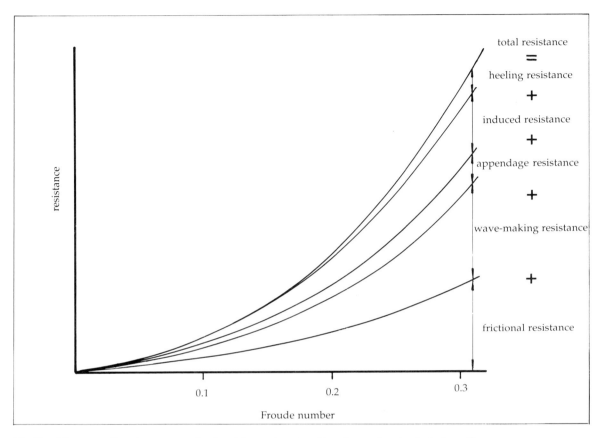

resistance

total resistance
=
heeling resistance
+
induced resistance
+
appendage resistance
+
wave-making resistance
+
frictional resistance

0.1   0.2   0.3

Froude number

Fig 91   The proportionate components of resistance, based on Froude number, typical of a sailing yacht.

the ease with which water, in this case, can flow over the surface. Surface roughness, therefore, must affect the value of the coefficient of friction.

However, even for a smooth-as-glass surface, frictional resistance occurs because the water is slowed close to the surface due to its contact with that surface. In fact, frictional resistance is unaffected up to a certain level of roughness, termed *critical roughness*, which for most (slowish) boats would be the roughness – or smoothness if you look at it that way – of a surface prepared with 400- or 600-grade wet and dry abrasive paper. We can regard the

surface quality as 'smooth' where the level of roughness is sub-critical.

Given that the bottom of a boat is smooth, the coefficient of friction depends upon Reynolds number. The principal variable upon which Reynolds number depends, other than velocity, is length, and it is of some interest to note that a long surface possesses less drag than a short surface of the same area.

This does assume that the flow over the surface is basically non-laminar. Laminar flow is indicated by 'layers' of the water flowing one over the other without disruption and occurs for a short distance aft of the leading edge, particularly at low speeds. More normal flow, where there is some disruption of the flow close to the surface, but no reverse flow, is termed *turbulent flow*.

A value for the coefficient of friction can be calculated from Reynolds number, and this therefore presents a theoretical means of predicting frictional resistance. This is unlike the coefficient of drag, which really can be found only by model testing.

Although the coefficient of friction for a smooth surface is based upon Reynolds number only, there is no universally agreed formula. Every now and again the leading experimenters, after much towing and measuring, meet to agree on modifications to existing formulae and to propose new ones.

One such formula which has stood the test of time follows, though perhaps I should warn readers of a nervous disposition or non-mathematical persuasion not to worry if it makes no sense:

$$C_F = \frac{0.075}{(\log_{10} Re - 2)^2}$$

Suppose the speedboat already discussed has a planing length of 4m which is used as a basis for Reynolds number, and a wetted surface area of 4.5m. At 7.105m/s, its coefficient of friction, using the formula above, would be 0.00258 and the frictional resistance a predicted 300N. This is a substantial 25 per cent of the total resistance, but can be considerably more. An important maxim is to minimize wetted surface area for the least frictional resistance (and it is important to keep the bottom smooth).

Frictional resistance is the only component which is readily calculable (well, perhaps without too much difficulty) and this is because we assume it depends upon area and length but not shape. The resistance of all the other elements varies with their form. Where shape counts, no easy formula to predict resistance can be proposed because it is difficult to define the shape in a mathematical way. For simplicity, we therefore resort to the testing of models.

Model Testing

Although it is a useful design tool, the model testing of hulls in specifically built test tanks is not routinely undertaken because of the high costs involved. For racing or innovative designs, model testing is valuable as an indicator of performance. But the use of models has led, on occasion, to designs which, though promising in the tank, perform badly at full size mainly due to the difficulty of duplicating conditions likely to be encountered (*see* Fig 92).

SUMMARY — THE COMPONENTS OF RESISTANCE

1   The resistance of a hull is equal to the propulsive force. Neglecting losses, the power required is given by the product of the propulsive force and the hull's velocity.

2   The proportion of each of the components of resistance to the total varies with velocity and the hull form. Heavy-displacement boats experience a large proportion of wave-making resistance at high velocities. Frictional resistance is significant for all craft at lower velocities.

3   Frictional resistance is the only component which can be calculated readily because it is largely independent of hull form.

Fig 92   Model testing can begin at an early age.

Fig 93   The carriage in a test tank before the lights go green.

The model, which ideally should be to as large a scale as the tank will allow, is towed by a carriage straddling the tank and travelling on rails (*see* Fig 93). The tank can be up to a kilometre in length in order to maintain constant speed for a reasonable period of time. Using *dynamometric* apparatus, the forces occurring on the model are measured electronically. The resistance, generally, is the most significant.

Scaling the resistance from the model to the full-sized craft involves splitting the resistance into the easily calculable part (the frictional resistance) and the other components which depend upon the form. These components (technically omitting air resistance) are grouped and termed *residual resistance*.

We can deduce the model's residual resistance by subtracting from the tested total resistance the calculated frictional resistance. The model's residual resistance then can be scaled to give the full-sized craft's residual resistance (we multiply by the scale cubed); since its frictional resistance can be calculated, the total resistance of the boat can be determined. This must be at the same Froude number because only then are the wave systems similar so that we can scale the residual resistance.

An example may make the procedure clearer. Suppose a one-sixth scale model of a displacement yacht of 10m length water-line is tested at 1.26m/s (2.44 knots) and its resistance is 6.56N (1.47lb). Suppose frictional resistance is calculated to be 2.50N, implying that residual resistance is 6.56 − 2.50 = 4.06N. The corresponding full-sized craft's velocity must be 3.09m/s for equality of Froude number. Residual resistance is $4.06 \times 6^3 = 877$N. The frictional resistance is calculated to be 334N and therefore we predict the total resistance to be 877 + 334 = 1211N at 3.09m/s (272lb at 6.0 knots). The steps are shown (*see* Fig 94).

A series of runs is made in the test tank, the resistance being measured at various velocities up to an expected maximum scale

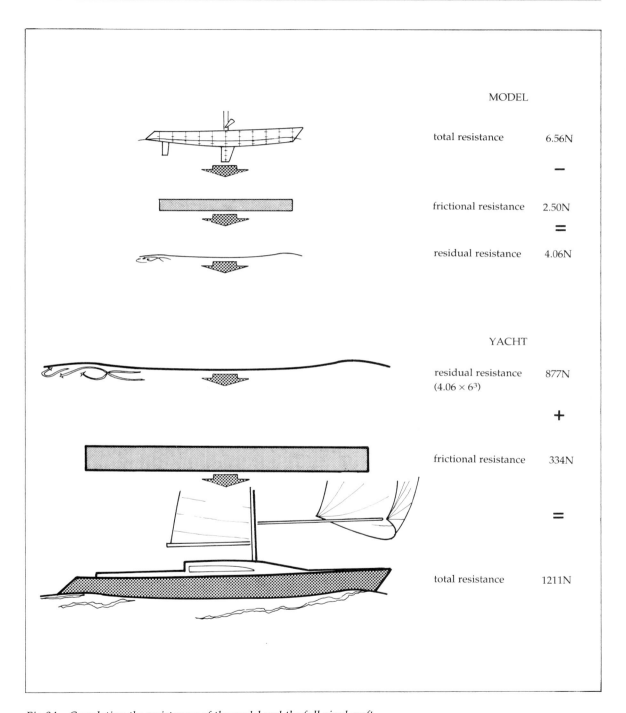

MODEL

total resistance   6.56N

–

frictional resistance   2.50N

=

residual resistance   4.06N

YACHT

residual resistance   877N
(4.06×6^3)

+

frictional resistance   334N

=

total resistance   1211N

Fig 94   Correlating the resistances of the model and the full-sized craft.

Figs 95(a–f)   *A natural test tank! The model is towed at increasing speed. The transition from displacement to planing mode is seen clearly. In the final photograph, resistance has increased even though the pointer indicates otherwise – a different scale was in use.*

Fig 95(a)

Fig 95(b)

Fig 95(c)

Fig 95(d)

Fig 95(e)

Fig 95(f)

velocity. For really high-speed craft, the carriage may need to be run as fast as the urban speed limit – and all done without seat belts! At each velocity the resistance of the full-sized craft is calculated and then graphed (*see* Figs 95 a–f).

The origins of this procedure are owed to William Froude as long ago as the 1870s. He recognized the need for separating frictional resistance from residual resistance because they each obey a different law. But there are those who do not regard them as laws at all.

There has been much disagreement over which formula should be used to calculate the coefficient of friction. Uncertainty has been fostered by variability – using standard models in different tests tanks – the classic example being the existence of minor levels of algae in the water of one tank which reduced frictional resistance by as much as 14 per cent on one occasion. The phenomenon was not uncovered for a number of years, and so

familiar became the researchers with the variability in their results that they named the gremlin in the tank 'Iris'!

Another potential failing in the formulation of the coefficient of friction is the assurance of appropriate flow conditions, that is to say turbulent flow over a smooth surface. Because of the relatively short length of the models in use, it is possible that laminar flow can exist over a large proportion, if not all, of the model's length. Laminar flow tends to be unstable, which makes it more difficult to predict the resulting frictional resistance.

In practice, turbulent flow is assured by disrupting the flow at the bow and the leading edges of the keel. Either trip-wires, sand strips or small studs are used. But whether or not this properly simulates the flow conditions for the full-sized craft is open to debate.

A more serious question mark over the validity of the tank testing of models is

Fig 96   A manoeuvring tank, complete with sandbanks and tides.

whether the dynamic operating conditions in which full-sized craft find themselves can be duplicated. Although waves can be created in the tank, the angle and nature of the waves meeting the hull may be poorly modelled. The model's response is also unlikely to be realistic as it operates at constant velocity during a run rather than at constant force.

Under the more or less constant propulsive force from an engine or the sails, velocity changes as waves pass under the boat. When travelling with the waves, the boat speeds up as it surfs on the crest, and then it slows in the trough. Similar variations occur when sailing or powering into the waves.

For these reasons, the behaviour of powered craft is often examined using manoeuvring tanks in which the model is operated by radio control or, if large enough, by carrying a 'helmsman'. This really is 'playing with boats'. A fair assessment can be made of behaviour in waves, in shallow water and with a tide running, but such tests tend not to be quantitive (*see* Fig 96).

Similarly, free-sailing models (*see* Fig 97) do not provide information of a numerical kind, but observation yields information about pitching and general behaviour in waves, dynamic characteristics when heeled and an indication of turning capabilities. Some designers prefer this approach anyway, as it's

Fig 97   A free-sailing model.

good to be close to the action and it improves sensibilities. The temperate, humid climate of the test tank with its dials and VDUs does little to clear the head.

SUMMARY — MODEL TESTING

1   Tank testing procedure includes measuring the resistance of the model at various velocities. By splitting the resistance into frictional and residual resistance, the resistance of the full-sized craft can be predicted at the same Froude number.

2   The potential limitations in tank testing lie in the questionable effectiveness of the system of prediction and the fact that the model is not operating in true dynamic conditions of waves and constant propulsive force.

3   Freely operating models offer an insight into general behaviour.

Chapter 4

About Sails, Foils and Things

Sail Design

Sails mostly come in twos, at least for smaller yachts and sailing dinghies. For larger yachts the sail plan is often divided into three or more sails for ease of handling. The sails I generally describe are those normally set and are suitable for sailing upwind. It may help to refer to Fig 98. Many yachts carry a plethora of sails of different sizes below deck, among which there usually will be a spinnaker. Spinnakers essentially are downwind sails but can be set with the wind on the beam, and are used by both yachts and dinghies (*see* Fig 99). Cruising sailors often scorn spinnakers because they are difficult to set, many preferring a hybrid sail which is a cross between a spinnaker and a jib, but which is set in the manner of a jib.

A proportion of sailing dinghies use a single sail and therefore are described as being *una rigged* or *cat rigged* (*see* Fig 100). Generally, these dinghies are designed to be sailed single-handed. Where two sails are employed, the rig is termed a *sloop rig* and comprises mainsail and jib (sometimes termed a headsail or, if it is large, a genoa) as in Fig 101. Universally, dinghies are three-quarter rigged, whereby the jib is set from the mast at about the three-quarter height position.

Most yachts currently are three-quarter rigged, though the term *fractional* is used generally for description because yachts vary quite widely in the height at which the jib or spinnaker are set (*see* Fig 102).

For a number of years, from the 1950s to the 1970s, a large number of yachts were designed with a masthead rig (*see* Fig 103). This sprung from the rules used to rate racing yachts, these rules assessing leniently the foretriangle area. It was of benefit to use a large foretriangle relative to the mainsail area because this proportion permitted a large spinnaker.

The trend towards masthead rigs spread to cruising yachts for no real reason other than the dictates of fashion, though rig simplicity was a bonus. The swing back to fractional rigs has resulted from much the same rule-oriented cause. A tax on foretriangle area has led to fractional rigs for rating-rule-led racing yachts, and those destined for the cruiser or club racing market have followed suit.

Fore and aft sails, that is those suitable for sailing upwind, are generally of triangular planform, the rig then being described as *bermudan*. Quadrilateral sails are rare. The gaff rig is the most prominent type, a gaff being used to support the upper edge of the sail (*see* Fig 104). Some triangular sails have a plan form which is somewhat quadrilateral, *battens* being used to project the sail. In mainsails, either three or four battens are used for the purpose of assisting the free edge to stand, particularly where it has substantial round (or *roach*).

Although it is the sailmaker's prerogative to design the cut of the sails so that they set well, the designer of the boat takes responsibility for the design of the sail plan. At that stage, the designer must decide upon not only the

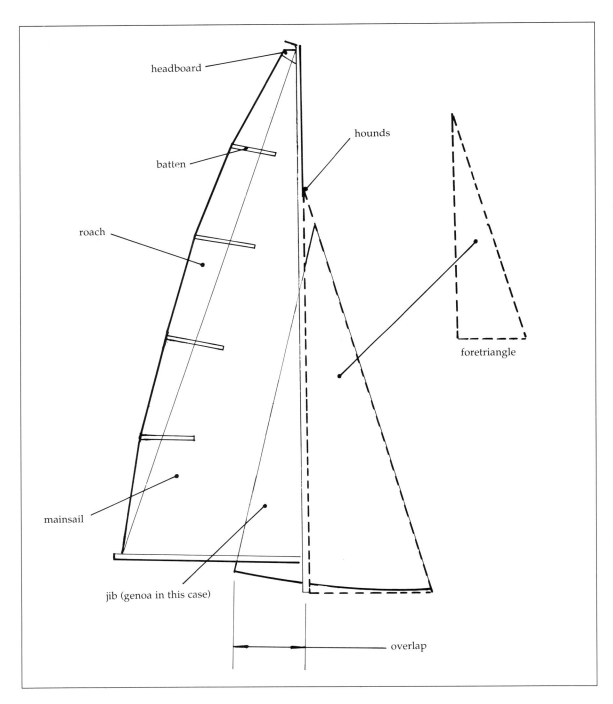

headboard

hounds

batten

roach

foretriangle

mainsail

jib (genoa in this case)

overlap

Fig 98   Terminology.

Fig 99 Spinnakers are getting lighter.

Fig 100 A una rig.

Fig 101 A sloop rig.

Fig 102 A fractional rig with foretriangle at ⁷⁄₈ height.

Fig 103   A masthead rig of a class of yacht
which made its mark in the seventies.

Fig 104   A gaff rig. An additional sail called a
topsail is set to provide extra area.

type of rig but also the height relative to width
of the sails, the area and the division of the sail
plan, the amount that the jib should overlap
the mainsail, and the choice of other sails for
the wardrobe, including the spinnaker.

The decision about the planform when considering downwind sailing is not especially
important. The maximum driving force comes
from the maximum area, and aspect ratio of
the sails is not especially significant. In one
respect, tall sails benefit from the wind gradient, which indicates a faster wind speed
with height above the sea. But then high aspect ratio spinnakers tend to be harder to set,
and downwind rolling is encouraged.

To windward, a high aspect ratio sail plan
has the disadvantage that the turbulence from
the mast on the mainsail, which is necessarily
narrow towards its head, leads to this part of
the sail being of low effectiveness. Thus, there

is value in extending the roach at the top of
the mainsail as much as the headboard and
battens will allow.

Fig 105 highlights the most effective part of
a typical mainsail when the boat is sailing to
windward with the sail at a fairly small angle
of attack. A high aspect ratio sail of the same
area is more effective than its low aspect ratio
counterpart in terms of the driving force it can
produce, particularly if the mast diameter is
small. It can be that a high aspect ratio sail
plan produces more driving force and yet less
heeling force, the latter offsetting the larger
heeling lever common to high aspect ratio sail
plans.

It may come as no surprise to find that the
position regarding the relative merits of high
and low aspect ratio is generally reversed
when the wind is abeam. In this case, lower
sail plans (see Fig 106) pay off because they

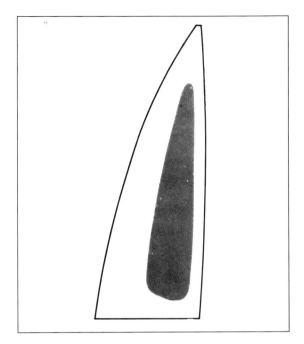

Fig 105   The most effective part of a mainsail.

Fig 106   A low aspect ratio sail.

produce more driving force. When sailing to windward, high lift–drag ratios are sought after. Off the wind, more driving force results from oversheeting somewhat and, at this larger angle of attack, low aspect ratio sails push you where you want to go.

Design often advances most quickly in the restricted or development racing classes where there is opportunity to try new ideas, usually within limits. Among those classes which permit freedom in the design of the sail plan, usually within the constraints of a maximum sail area and height, various trends emerge. Most significantly, except for very high-speed craft, sloop rigs appear to be more effective than una rigs.

The other significant features are the use of high aspect ratio for both mainsail and jib, a reasonable roach in the mainsail especially towards the head, and a jib which does not over-lap (or only overlaps a little) the mainsail. The advantages of the first two features have been discussed already, but the third seems more controversial because most yachts and dinghies use substantial overlap. Such sails usually are referred to as *genoas*.

Amongst yachts, both for racing and cruising, as much as 55 per cent of the genoa often lies abaft the mast. Genoas came into being as a means of increasing sail area within the confines of the rig, but among racing off-shore yachts the use of overlap is rating rule led. Genoas are allowed under the rules to have this much overlap without penalty, and any less overlap provides no bonus. Designers of racing yachts do not turn down free sail area.

Two or three decades ago, sailing people spoke in hushed tones about genoas. It was as if something mystical occurred when this sail went up. A sailing adventure story of the era would have had the hero hoisting his genoa, lovingly ironed by his mother the night before, on the last leg of the race to win the coveted cup. Before about 1960, sails were made from cotton, the genoa being of a lighter weight cloth which was soft to handle, but prone to stretching out of shape.

The area on the boat between the genoa and the mainsail acquired a reverence, and anyone sitting, standing or otherwise lurking on this sacred ground would be castigated with shouts of 'get out of the slot!'. It was believed that any obstruction in this area substantially slowed the boat. Everyone who sailed seriously was convinced that the overlap of the genoa furnished a venturi which caused a funnelling and hence speeding up of the air flow in the slot.

More recent theory overturns this somewhat, it being suggested that less air flows through the slot. Instead, it is argued that the mainsail serves to encourage more air to flow to the lee side of the headsail which then becomes more effective. Therefore, this is the area which should be kept free from extraneous bodies.

This thinking leads towards the possibility of the mainsail and jib combination being regarded as a single aerofoil when sailing upwind (*see* Fig 107). On a total area basis, it is seen that the sail plan with overlap presents a

smaller single aerofoil than does a jib with no overlap. If a substantial gap is created between the jib and mainsail (perhaps it could be described as a negative overlap), the principle of the single aerofoil would have no merit because each sail would operate independently.

It seems logical that if two sails in combination are effective, three or more should be also. Ketch rigs, which tack on an additional sail similar to but smaller than the mainsail, called a mizzen, are a success in some circumstances but not in others. When the wind is free, ketch rigs work well. To windward the mizzen's effectiveness even in bolstering the other sails appears small. The necessity for placing the leading edge of all sails on the centreline of the yacht is a disadvantage – the mizzen could benefit the rig more if it were placed to windward slightly. In general, multiple foils (including sloop rigs) when arranged for best effect produce high values of lift but the drag tends to be higher than for a single sail.

For yachts where there is a freedom to set sails to choice in the foretriangle, the sail wardrobe is influenced by sail combination theory. Past practice has been to use jibs of the same proportions but of smaller size when there is a need to carry less sail in stronger winds. But it makes sense as a first step to use

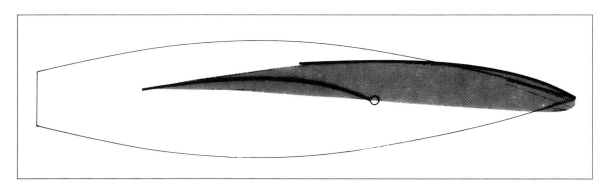

Fig 107   The possibility of the mainsail and jib being regarded as a single aerofoil.

SUMMARY — SAIL DESIGN

1   Yachts designed to rating rules have adopted, at different times, masthead or fractional rigs with a large genoa overlap. Cruising yachts have tended to follow suit.

2   Sailing to windward benefits from the use of a high aspect ratio sail plan, and reaching from a low aspect ratio sail plan.

3   It is now supposed that the mainsail encourages air to flow to leeward of the jib, which thinking is, to an extent, contrary to the 'slot theory'. Genoa overlap is a less effective part of the sail plan.

4   Sloop rigs are effective for boats of normal speed, but high-speed craft benefit from a una rig.

a jib having less overlap but of the same hoist. This eliminates the part of the sail which is least useful because it produces a disproportionate amount of heeling force relative to driving force.

Performance Prediction

Some researchers within the discipline of sail aerodynamics believe that the soul of the sail plan can only be revealed by measuring the forces produced by the actual sails in action. One approach is to tether the rig so that the forces can be measured directly without going afloat. This sounds good for armchair researchers. Another approach is by using strain gauges on the rigging under sailing conditions. I have to say that some yachtsmen, and designers for that matter, believe that souls should not be scrutinized, that genoas are genoas and that researchers should be tethered to their armchairs.

However, if you are of a mind, it is of value to use the data gathered by researchers for the purposes of design. The underlying principle in the use of such data is that a sail plan of twice the area but of similar shape should produce forces all of which are twice as great, with some provisos. For ease of measurement,

model sail plans are often tested, the forces being reduced to coefficient form. The coefficients established are the coefficient of lift C_L and the coefficient of drag C_D, both being based on the surface area of one side of the sail.

For example, under test a model sail including mast and rigging might indicate the following coefficients at the angles of attack α (Greek letter alpha) measured. The lift–drag ratio has also been calculated because this provides an important measure of efficiency. This was calculated from C_L and C_D, as the ratio of these is the same as the ratio of lift and drag.

α^0	C_L	C_D	lift-drag ratio
10	1.02	0.25	4.08
15	1.52	0.40	3.80
20	1.27	0.53	2.40
25	1.21	0.61	1.98
30	1.17	0.69	1.70
40	0.96	0.81	1.19
50	0.80	0.96	0.83
60	0.66	1.08	0.61
70	0.50	1.20	0.42
80	0.29	1.31	0.22
90	0.00	1.35	0.00

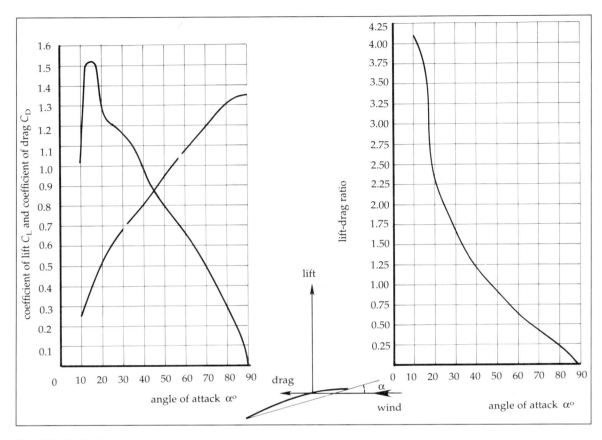

Fig 108   Sail data.

For clarity this information can be represented on a graph (*see* Fig 108).

Although this data is realistic for an efficient rig, it will provide a means of accurately finding the forces on a chosen rig only if there is similarity with the model's sail plan, in particular with regard to aspect ratio, the shape of the roach, the degree of mast and rigging interference for a mainsail, *camber* (or belly), and of course the interaction if there is more than one sail. Suppose we have a sail just like the one used to produce this data. Its area is 10m² (108 ft²) and the angle at which it is set to the wind, blowing at 5m/s (9.7 knots), is 15 degrees. We note that C_L is 1.52 and C_D is 0.40. Now the lift force:

$$F_L = \frac{1}{2} \times \rho \times a \times v^2 \times C_L$$
$$= \frac{1}{2} \times 1.225 \times 10 \times 5 \times 1.52$$
$$= 233N$$

and the drag force:

$$F_D = \frac{1}{2} \times \rho \times a \times v^2 \times C_D$$
$$= \frac{1}{2} \times 1.225 \times 10 \times 5^2 \times 0.40$$
$$= 61N.$$

These forces may not seem high, but then the sail is small and the wind is not strong. The lift–drag ratio in comparison with an asymmetrical foil having thickness is also low. This results not only from the sail's lack of thickness and from the drag produced by the mast and rigging, but also because the foil is able to operate at smaller angles of attack than the sail, when high lift-drag ratios are obtained.

So, providing the designer has the information to produce such graphs as in Fig 108, he can derive the magnitude and direction of the forces produced by his chosen rig at various wind speeds and at various angles of attack.

For a sloop rig, the coefficients of lift and drag may be expressed for the combination of mainsail and jib rather than for each sail independently. When sailing sufficiently broad to the wind, the combination becomes the mainsail and spinnaker. The coefficients of single mainsail, mainsail and jib, and mainsail and spinnaker will each be different. This reflects the variation in efficiency between each set-up, the coefficients representing the particular force per unit area.

The figures presented relate to the wind and the rig regardless of the hull. We now can consider the rig placed on a hull. In practice, the problem is approached from the opposite direction. That is to say, the angle of the boat to the wind is selected and then the sail or sails are sheeted (theoretically) to the best angle. There are ways in which the angle of attack for maximum driving force can be found, but for simplicity I suggest that this angle is chosen as one might sheet a sail. Also, for simplicity, the difference between the actual wind and the felt wind has been by-passed, and this will be discussed later.

The total force F_T can be shown diagramatically, from which the driving force F_R (the subscript R is used to avoid confusion with the drag force) is found. F_R is the force pushing the boat in the direction it sails, and the higher this force the better. The force to be minimized is the heeling force F_H. Its value usually is found in order to calculate the angle of heel.

Both the driving force and the heeling force

can be calculated or computed, but it is simple enough to draw all the forces to scale in the directions in which they act. Fig 109 best shows how F_R and F_H are measured to scale to reveal the magnitude of these forces. The angle at which the boat sails to the wind, in this case it is 50 degrees, dictates the values of F_R and F_H. These are 139N and 196N respectively.

This sets the stage for a *performance prediction*, which for a sailing boat is a forecast of its speed at various angles to the wind. The driving force when on a close reach has been calculated to be 139N when the wind is at 50 degrees to the course sailed. We next need the resistance curve for the boat. The section on model testing covers the way in which this curve is derived. When the resistance is 139N, the same as the driving force, we can read from the curve the boat speed. This is our prediction, therefore, of the boat's speed in that wind strength and at that angle to the wind. The process is then repeated for a number of angles to the wind to present an overall picture of performance.

Although the stage may have been set, the plot thickens. For the performance prediction to receive rave reviews, allowance must be made for the reduction in efficiency of the sail plan and hull on heeling; the leeway or side slip of the hull; and the difference between the apparent wind (the wind felt on board, its speed and direction) and the true wind (the actual wind).

Some amplification of the last point is called for. In the example given, the forces were based upon an apparent wind of 5m/s and 50 degrees from the course sailed. Since the boat would have been sailing to some extent towards the wind, the true wind would be of lower speed and at a larger angle. The problem is circular and complex. If we start with a known true wind, we don't know how fast the boat will go because we cannot work out the speed and direction of the apparent wind,

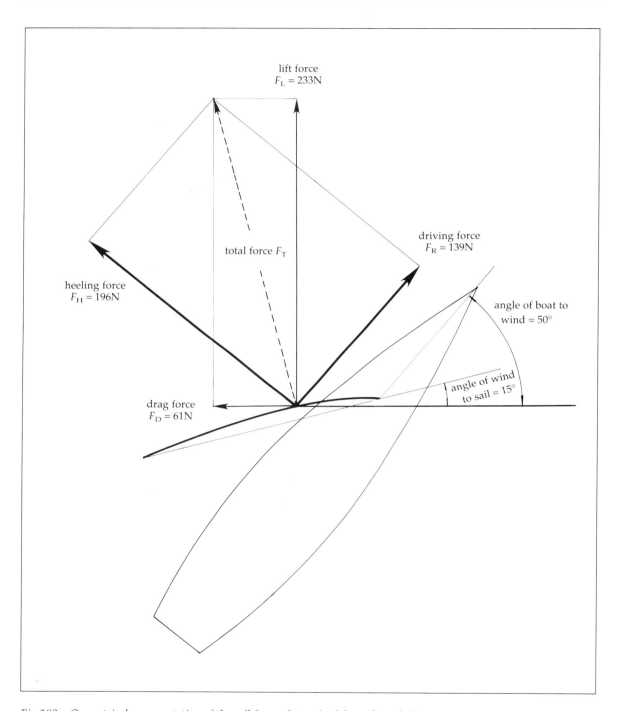

Fig 109   Geometrical representation of the sail forces determined from the sail data.

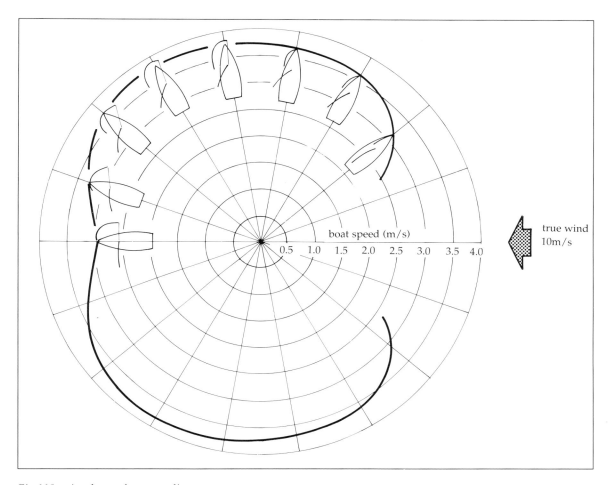

boat speed (m/s)

0.5 1.0 1.5 2.0 2.5 3.0 3.5 4.0

true wind
10m/s

Fig 110   A polar performance diagram.

which is affected by how fast the boat will go. If you understand that on first reading then you may go to the end of the book and collect your diploma.

In practice, the circle is broken by jumping in with both deck shoes, that is by guessing the boat speed. You then go around the circle to see how good your guess was so that you can improve on it until everything fits.

We then go and repeat this for a number of angles to the true wind. The output is a rela-tively simple one considering the complexity of the process. For a given wind strength and a range of angles to the boat's centreline, we obtain the boat's speed at each angle. This in-formation is often displayed on a performance diagram of a polar kind (*see* Fig 110). A series of performance diagrams can be produced for several wind strengths.

SUMMARY — PERFORMANCE PREDICTION

1   The testing of sail plans either at full size or to scale establishes the coefficients of lift and drag at various angles of attack. This data can be used to predict the sail forces on a chosen rig provided there is similarity of form and of Reynolds number.

2   The sails can be thought to be sheeted on a hull (for a simple approach) and the driving and heeling forces found.

3   Allowance for the apparent wind should be made, which creates complexity. The driving force equates with the resistance given by a resistance-velocity curve, leading towards the construction of a polar performance diagram indicating the boat's velocity at different angles to the wind.

Keel Design

Sailing boats do not work too well without a centreboard, daggerboard, leeboard or keel. When sailing upwind, dinghies make progress of a sort, but drift badly sideways away from the wind. Yachts also make a large amount of leeway, but worse, they fall over. Multihulls manage best because the hulls, generally, are narrow and deep.

Although the two requirements of minimizing leeway and improving stability are primary, other factors may be of importance. For instance, a yacht for deep-sea cruising might be best suited with a long keel having a large surface area (*see* Fig 111). This type of keel damps motion which is good for seaworthiness. It also leads to a high level of directional stability. This is good for cruising since it is possible to leave the helm for reasonable lengths of time.

Yachts of this type, with a long keel of large lateral area, usually make only a small amount of leeway because the keel works well to resist it. Low values of leeway are to be prized because when a boat is sailing upwind, leeway takes it away from its target.

Now, if a large keel is good for reducing leeway, then surely a keel the size of a billboard would be better? Well, no, it would not

be. Firstly, there is a law of diminishing returns. Secondly, the wetted area and hence surface frictional resistance would be gross. This, in fact, is the main drawback for long-keeled boats, which suffer particularly in light winds when surface frictional drag is a significant proportion of the total resistance. And thirdly, no one is going to pay for advertising space under the water.

For every hundred metres a boat travels forwards, it crabs sideways about five metres. Actually, this is reasonably efficient. Chop off the keel, use all the bodies in the gymnasium on rugby night for stability, and the typical yacht would drift perhaps fifteen or twenty metres in every hundred.

Generally, leeway is expressed as an angle. Thus, a typical five metres down the slippery slope in a hundred metres would represent nearly 3 degrees of leeway. Angles of leeway generally range between 3 and 6 degrees, the latter being typical for a yacht using shallow twin keels (often called bilge keels) as illustrated in Fig 112.

The hull does its bit in the fight against leeway, but the keel constitutes the main artillery. It operates as a foil, that is as a lift device, its angle of attack being the same as the angle of leeway. At least, this would be true under

Fig 111   A long-keeled yacht.

Fig 112   Bilge keels.

steady state conditions. Variations in wind and particularly waves produce severe accelerations and this means that the keel's view of its world keeps changing.

At one instant, the keel's angle of attack might be 3 degrees, then it might be 12 degrees, then –4 degrees and so on. When the angle of attack is an unstable 12 degrees, stalling is likely to occur. This has been examined by one experimenter who spent time looking through clear plastic in the hull's bottom at a keel while the boat and he were plunging, rolling and heaving in a seaway. Whether or not the keel was stalling was determined by the behaviour of lengths of thread attached to the keel. It was found that the thread suffered major disturbance, indicating stalling, up to 20 per cent of the time. Worse, when the keel stalled the flow was not re-established for as much as a boat length travelled.

In the days when centreboards were plates of steel, daggerboards were rectangles of plywood with the edges chamfered and keels looked as though they had been cast in a bath, stalling must have been rife. The leading edge,

if angular or bluff, can easily lead to a local breakdown of flow which initiates stalling (*see* Fig 113). Ideally, the leading edge of a foil should be of a section that enables the water to change direction gradually. *Parabolic* sections do this because the curvature changes progressively. Sharp entries produce less drag under steady state conditions with zero angle of attack, but the flow breaks down readily in the conditions to which a keel is subjected.

Choosing the shape of the section of the keel (the section being a horizontal cutting plane) is a Difficult Design Decision. This is not through a lack of information but because of a plethora of data. Most significant in the delineation of possible sections and their characteristics is NACA, the National Advisory Committee for Aeronautics.

Don't be put off by the thought that aeronautics have nothing to do with keels. Although NACA's business is to do with aircraft, some juggling connected with Reynolds numbers means that the data is applicable below the waves. Also, don't think that, being a committee, the front end of an aerofoil is

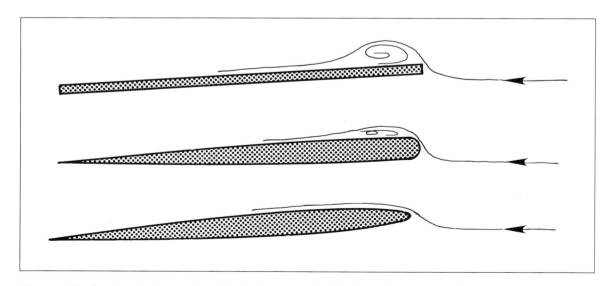

Fig 113   The flow breaks down readily at the leading edge of a foil where there are discontinuities.

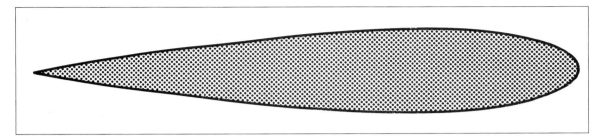

Fig 114   NACA 0015.

agreed upon one day and the back end the next, with bids being made for the lift and drag characteristics.

In fact, NACA now is replaced by NASA, but the memory and work of NACA live on in the amazingly numerous and diverse sections tested and catalogued. A fair number have no application for keels. The asymmetrical aerofoils have no relevance because, while the boat would be awesome on one tack, it would be a pudding on the other. Mind you, a keel which changes shape like a bendy toy or articulates in sections is reality enough.

NACA present families of sections with certain common characteristics. For example, NACA's 0006, 0009, 0012 and 0015 are basically the same section but of increasing thickness (*see* Fig 114). The last two digits indicate the percentage of the section's thickness to its length, that is, the distance between the leading and trailing edges, the length being known as the *chord length*. For example, a dinghy centreboard of 400mm chord length shaped to NACA 0006 would have a thickness which is 6 per cent of 400mm, that is, 24mm. The first two digits refer to the section's camber or degree of asymmetry, which in this case is zero.

This series of sections has always been regarded as good, if conservative. The form is a basic streamlined one, maximum fullness being 30 per cent aft of the leading edge. Having the fullness this far forward leads to generalized turbulent flow which is stable.

This means that while drag is not especially low, neither does it rise alarmingly at times, and the sections are fairly resistant to stalling. Anti-stalling characteristics improve with the thicker sections, the 0006 coping with an angle of attack of 8 or 9 degrees, the 0009 managing up to 11 or 12 degrees, and so on. Against this, there is more drag for the thicker sections. This is a real drag, especially downwind for a keel boat, when the keel is not required to produce lift.

Keel boats often use thicker-sectioned keels because of the need to build in the required amount of ballast, 15 per cent sections sometimes being called for. Despite the reality that the keel can be stalled for as much as one-fifth of the time in a seaway, the pursuit of performance has led to the use of lower drag but more sensitive sections. This type of section tends to stall more readily because the entry is sharper. The maximum thickness is about 40 per cent aft of the leading edge, the aim being that laminar flow will exist back to this point.

These NLF (natural laminar flow) sections have low drag because laminar flow causes substantially less drag than turbulent flow. An example of these is the so-called 6 series NACA sections which are 'designer' sections in that they are a design cocktail for a specific purpose, such as the 63_2–015 (*see* Fig 115). The 6 indicates the series, the 3 that maximum velocity occurs 30 per cent aft, the first zero that there is no camber (i.e. it is a symmetrical

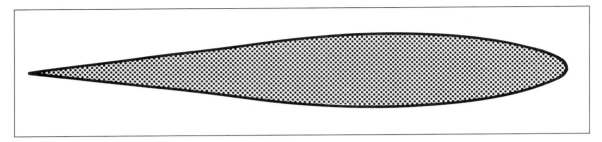

Fig 115   NACA 63$_2$–015.

section), and the 15 that the thickness-chord length ratio is 15 per cent. The subscript 2 is indicative of the width of the low drag bucket (*see* Fig 116). If you are wondering how buckets can have low drag, just think of this as a funny number invented by not very funny people just to complicate things for you and me.

More extreme laminar flow sections have

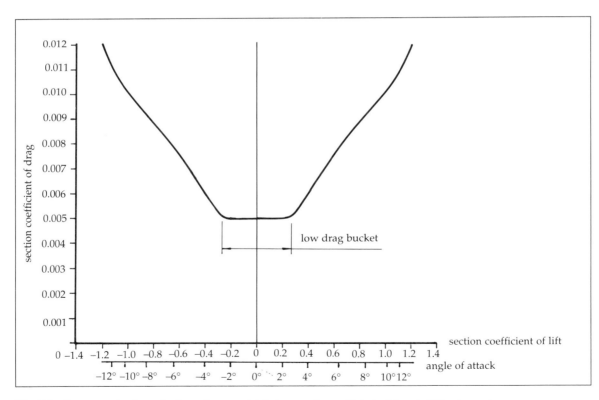

Fig 116   For an angle of attack of zero to around ± 2 degrees, the coefficient of drag is little changed, this region represented by the curve being termed the low drag bucket because of its typical shape.

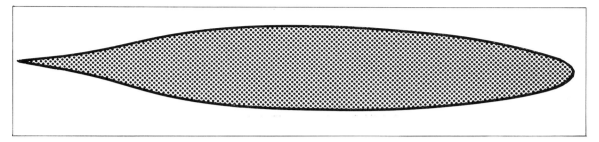

Fig 117   Laminarity is sustained over a large proportion of the foil.

been developed and do have potential (*see* Fig 117). The main feature of these sections is that the maximum thickness is located a long way aft of the leading edge in the hope that laminarity can be sustained back to this position. The drawback is that laminarity is temperamental and can suddenly be lost in the right (or wrong) conditions. When this occurs, a bubble is formed and the drag is greater at this time than for any foil you would think of using. For the laminar sections, the flow conditions around the keel tend to be poor at a Reynolds number of around one million, equivalent to about 1.1m/s (2.2 knots) for a keel foil of chord length of 1m. Laminar separation can be avoided by employing turbulence inducers on the surface just aft of the point of maximum thickness.

The sections described by NACA are defined by a series of precise offsets for the accurate cutting of foils. Some people, however, believe that a tenth of a millimetre or even a millimetre or more makes little odds, particularly as the choice of section has a swings and roundabouts feel about it. Some people believe that the choice of a section is not a Difficult Design Decision but just Simple Guesswork and are happy to use a JPGP section (Jack Plane and Glass Paper) for a dinghy centreboard, or an LHCC section (Lump Hammer and Cold Chisel) for a keel, there being an infinite number of sections in each series!

In fact, it pays to take a plane or cold chisel to the trailing edge of the centreboard or keel. Cutting back the sharp edge to produce a flat, with a width approaching 10 per cent of the foil thickness, improves the lift by as much as 10 percent, with a negligible increase in drag.

The wide range of planforms used for keels also supports the argument that no one has all the answers, or at least that one keel may perform well in one circumstance but be outshone by another keel in different conditions. In general, high aspect ratio keels perform well. Of course, high aspect ratio equates with a deep keel of small chord length and there could be attendant problems of deep draught with shallow water, and low keel volume for ballast mass.

Because the keel operates at a low angle of attack, a high aspect ratio generally is the most efficient. The leading edge is the most profitable lift-producing area of the keel when the angle of attack is small, because under this flow condition the differential in pressure matters most. High aspect ratio implies high lift and a high lift-drag ratio (*see* Fig 118).

It has been thought that if the length of the leading edge is important, then the use of a large sweep back in the keel (*see* Fig 119) must enhance lift. But the aspect ratio is unchanged for the same draught, and the sweep back increases the induced drag (which results from the production of lift). Sweep back encourages

105

Fig 118   A high aspect ratio keel. Drying out must be fun.

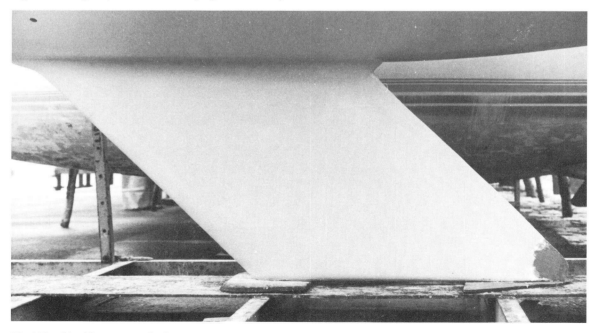

Fig 119   Significant sweep back.

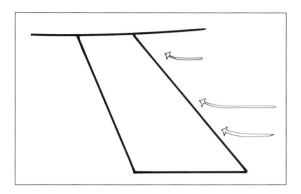

Fig 120   A forward-swept keel. A more regular loading results from increasing the chord at the bottom.

the water to flow downwards and this increases the water loading on the keel towards the bottom. The bottom of the keel, therefore, is likely to stall earlier than the rest of the keel. Least induced drag occurs with only slight sweep back.

A reduction in the chord length of the bottom of the keel reduces the loading, and so it makes sense to design a backswept keel with a greater chord at the top than at the bottom. The converse would apply to a forward-swept keel (see Fig 120).

Much work has been done in the aircraft field (or, more correctly, in the wind tunnel) with respect to the loading distribution of

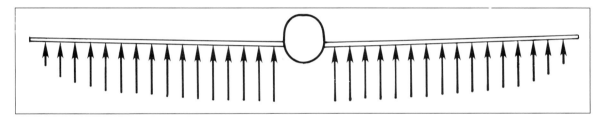

Fig 121   Elliptical loading.

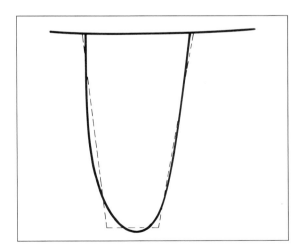

Fig 122   The trapezoidal plan form, shown by the dotted line, performs similarly to the elliptical keel.

wings. It is reasoned and has been shown that the wing is most efficient if the loading is highest at the fuselage end of the wing, and then reduces towards the tip, as in Fig 121. The loading distribution is seen to be elliptical, and it follows that an elliptical planform meets this requirement, though a tapered trapezoidal form is not greatly different (see Fig 122).

Elliptical keels are well suited to dinghies, but on yachts which lack human ballast and therefore tend to be well heeled in fresh winds, the pressure changes in the vicinity of the keel disrupt the water surface, and this increases resistance. One solution is to reduce the chord length of the keel at its root. This leads to planforms which resemble the shape of a petal (see Fig 123).

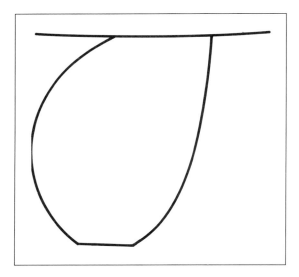

Fig 123   A plan form possibility for displacement yachts.

The shape of the bottom of the foil affects lift and induced drag. If the keel is long (which is good for taking the bottom without the yacht tipping), vortices result from the water flowing from high to low pressure round the bottom of the keel. Foil efficiency is improved by minimizing this tendency.

Two main approaches can be adopted. The first is to do away with the part that causes the problem, for example by using an elliptical or tapered plan form to the bottom of the foil. The second is to design the foil to obstruct the vortex. Either wings or a bulb located at the bottom of the keel are effective in this, and keep the ballast low in a ballast keel (*see* Fig 124).

Wings were a big hit on yachts of the Twelve Metre class used for the America's Cup competition. These beasts have a re-

Fig 124   Large wings on a six-metre yacht's keel.

Fig 125   Wings located above the bottom of the keel ease the problem of taking the ground.

stricted draught and the wings compensate for this. For this reason, wings do suit cruisers, especially as they damp a boat's movement in waves. The biggest disadvantage is when taking the bottom if it is sloping or rocky (*see* Fig 125). Fitting wings to a dinghy's daggerboard could also make it difficult to pull through the slot!

SUMMARY — KEEL DESIGN

1   The primary function of keels, centreboards and their variants is to limit leeway, and as such they behave as foils. The angle of attack may vary widely in a seaway, leading to stalling.

2   Thick sections having a parabolic entry with maximum fullness relatively far forward are most resistant to stalling. Laminar flow sections produce low drag under certain conditions.

3   Slight sweepback plus an elliptical planform produce minimal end losses and low induced drag. Wings located at the bottom of keels also minimize end losses and suit shallow draught yachts.

Rudder Design

Even if you still have your L-plates on the bow and stern, you will have some idea about how a rudder justifies its existence. But, like most matters nautical (especially design), there is more to rudders than meets the eye. We have come a large number of sea miles since the days when boats were steered using a crude oar on the larboard (now port) side.

In fact, the rudder has two separate functions to perform. Firstly, it must be able to hold the boat on course and, secondly, it must turn the boat effectively. These two requirements may seem to be one and the same, but they do result in subtle differences in rudder design.

Both requirements are served by the water meeting the rudder at an angle and producing a lift force (see Fig 126). This must sound familiar. For the rudder to do its job, it must be located towards, at, or beyond one end of the boat. If the rudder were located amidships it would move the boat crab-wise when

angled, rather than produce a turning effect (see Fig 127). Thus, the rudder should be positioned as far from the boat's 'pivoting' point (which usually is around or just forward of amidships) as possible. Some boats, both sail and power, even mount the rudder on a framework aft of the transom to magnify the effect.

It may seem surprising that a rudder placed at the bow would be serviceable. The only real difference is that, in this position on the boat, the helm is opposite to that for a conventional stern rudder (see Fig 128). Bow rudders operate in undisturbed water which is good for control, and any added sweepback tends to lift the bow when the rudder is applied, which acts as an anti-bow-burying measure.

Much of what I have said about keels, and also sails for that matter, applies to rudders, with regard to aspect ratio, sectional shape and plan form. The major way in which a rudder differs from a keel is that often it is called upon to work at very large angles of attack. Helmsmen tend to get a bit frantic when the

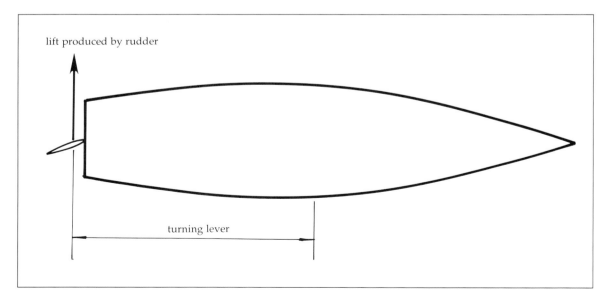

lift produced by rudder

turning lever

Fig 126   Rudders are foils too.

Fig 127   A rudder in this position has a small turning effect.

boat under them wants desperately to round up because of the wind or the waves. At times like these, helmsmen have little thought for hydrodynamic theory.

The situation is very similar to driving round a corner too fast when the road is wet. There may be some part of the brain which knows that turning the steering wheel further or applying more helm will make matters even worse, but instinct, or blind panic, over-rules reason. It has been suggested that squaring off the planform of the rudder at the bottom gives some warning of stall (*see* Fig 129) and I believe tyres are designed to give a

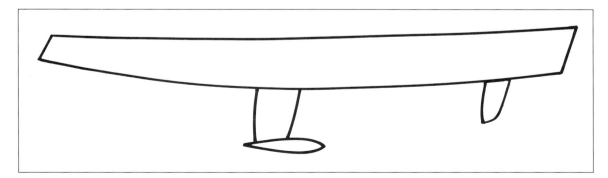

Fig 128   Forward rudders are feasible.

111

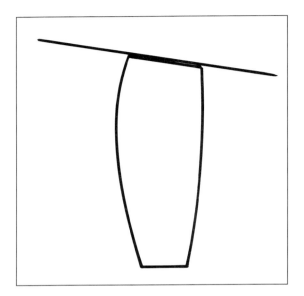

Fig 129   A possible rudder plan form.

Fig 130   A rudder with a high aspect ratio of four.

similar warning of sliding, though I can't see how square tyres help!

One approach adopted to minimize stalling is to duct water from the high pressure to the low pressure side and to the trailing edge of the rudder, thus 'regenerating' the separated water. This also smacks of tyre technology where water is fed from the tread outwards, in this case to minimize aquaplaning.

The point at which stalling occurs is affected in part by aspect ratio. In recent years, rudders have become of higher aspect ratio, especially for sailing craft, figures of four to six not being unusual (*see* Fig 130). (For a rectangular blade, this would be four or six times as deep as it is wide.) While performance is excellent at smaller angles of attack, high aspect ratio rudders do stall earlier than their low aspect ratio counterparts, and this can be a major disadvantage.

When totally stalled, rudders based on different sections all produce similar lift and large amounts of drag. The amount of lift is less than when the rudder is in the pre-stalled condition. In conclusion, the rudder should be designed so that stalling is delayed as long as possible with increasing helm, and this requires the use of a thick, streamlined section of about 12 to 15 per cent thickness to chord length ratio. Thin sections, even if streamlined, are less effective because a separation bubble will form at smaller angles of attack due to the finer entry, and this precipitates stalling.

Against this, jumbo sections do have more drag when not called upon to produce lift, that is, when trailing. Rudders spend a fair proportion of their time in this position, although if you watch a helmsman at work on a boat with tiller steering sailing to windward, the tiller, and therefore rudder, really are being worked. You may have to catch your helmsman while he is not looking because he is probably well aware that unwarranted rudder movement slows the boat.

One design philosophy is that full-sectioned rudders should be used not only because they produce high lift at large angles of attack, but because they occupy a greater volume than do thinner-sectioned rudders. A fair proportion of the total displacement is carried in the rudder with full sections and as a drag-producing body it is more efficient than the hull. But the effect is only really measurable for lightweight sailing dinghies and rated yachts for which lifting the stern out of the water at measurement benefits rating.

An alternative strategy in rudder design to delay stalling is simply to make the planform larger. This ensures that more lift is produced such that a smaller rudder angle is required to keep the boat on course. One starting point used to determine the area of the rudder is to relate it to the area of the *lateral plane* (*see* Fig 131) on the premise that the larger the lateral plane, the larger should be the rudder. In round numbers, for sailing yachts, 10 per cent is typical, while for sailing dinghies a figure of

15 per cent is common. Motor craft cope with a meagre 5 per cent. Guides of this kind can easily become too prescriptive – it is important to understand the principles and the conditions under which a rudder is expected to work.

High-speed craft require smaller rudders because the lift force increases as the square of velocity. The section should also be of a laminar type, that is, with the maximum fullness well aft, and the higher the speed the thinner the section should be. The full sections so praised for low-speed work cause a separation bubble at the leading edge, the water being unable to contour around the foil.

A propeller operating directly in front of the rudder increases the local water velocity and so powered craft can usually manage with a smaller rudder area (*see* Fig 132). It is usual to use a rudder behind each propeller, all rudders being linked so that they turn simultaneously. For multiple rudder installations, the total area can be thought to be divided.

Generally, especially for larger craft, the rudder is positioned inboard under the hull. Sealing the gap between the rudder and hull improves markedly the lift characteristics,

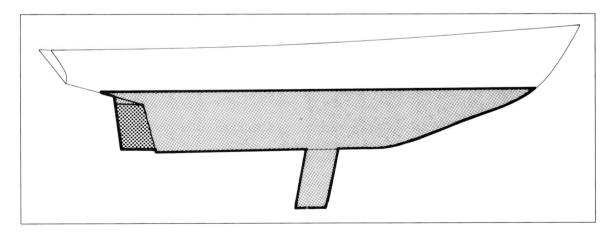

Fig 131   Rudder area often is related to the area of the lateral plane.

Fig 132   Only a small rudder area is required because of the increased water flow from the propeller.

Fig 133   A solution to placing the rudder under the hull without losing the lifting facility.

having basically the same function as wings on the bottom of keels. For dinghies and some yachts, the rudder is transom hung. The fact that the rudder passes through the water surface causes a problem known as *ventilation*. When the rudder is applied, the lowered water pressure causes air from the surface to ventilate downwards, thus reducing lift.

The way this is prevented, or at least minimized, is by building one or more horizontal *fences* into the rudder, close to the water surface. Fences are like small wings and look very racey, a definite plus for the go-fast brigade.

For those who do not like to be seen straining at the tiller, a *balanced* rudder is essential. The principle is to pivot the rudder somewhere close to the centre of force, which means that a part of the blade will lie ahead of the pivot point. The positioning of the pivot is everything. Get it wrong and the tiller could wrench violently out of the helmsman's grip and bury itself in his ribcage.

Getting it right is easy for high aspect ratio foils for which the centre of pressure varies only between about 20 and 24 per cent of the chord aft of the leading edge, the former percentage relating to the centre of pressure at small angles of attack and the latter to the position at stall. A suitable location for the pivot which provides adequate 'feel' for the helmsman and a self-centring action is around 16 per cent for an aspect ratio of five (*see* Fig 134).

Aspect ratios in the order of one (indicating a rudder as wide as it is deep) produce much greater variance. Tests indicate the forwardmost position to be 12 per cent, and at stall the centre of pressure lies 33 per cent aft. A suitable position for the pivot point, therefore, is some 9 per cent aft (*see* Fig 135) which does mean that, at large angles, the helm will be heavy.

If a boat is designed with a balanced rudder, a skeg positioned directly in front of the rudder is not feasible. A skeg is often used to

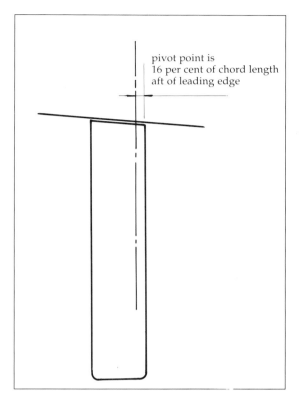

Fig 134 Pivot point for a high aspect ratio rudder.

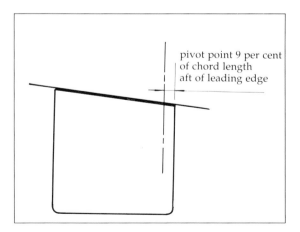

Fig 135 The pivot point must be further forward on a low aspect ratio rudder.

minimize the risk of structural failure, but it also has the advantage that the stall angle is increased by about 10 per cent (*see* Fig 136). At small angles of attack, the section produced by the skeg plus rudder is not unlike that used for an aircraft wing, the camber encouraging high lift (*see* Fig 137).

However, like most aspects of design, there is a downside. A skegged rudder is excellent for keeping a boat on course, but, for turning, the skeg is a positive hindrance. When turning, the bow swings one way and the stern, though wanting to swing the other, is obstructed by the skeg, so the speed of the turn is reduced. The same effect is noticed for long-keeled yachts which really do not like budging from the groove in which they sail.

The Conventional Approach to Sailing Balance

Sailboards manage very nicely without rudders. The board is steered mainly by moving the sail around. For example, when the sail is

Fig 136   A rudder with skeg.

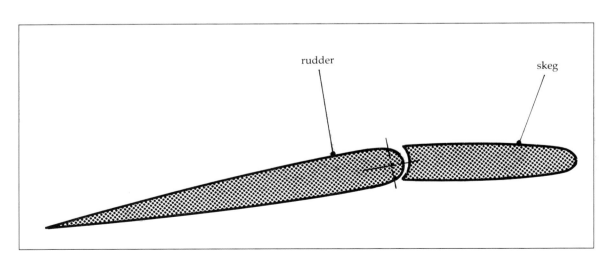

Fig 137   The section of the skeg and rudder combination is similar to an asymmetrical foil.

116

SUMMARY — RUDDER DESIGN

1   As a foil operating often at large angles of attack, the rudder should be of a section which is resistant to stalling. High aspect ratio planforms are efficient but are prone to early stalling.

2   Balanced rudders require a pivot forward of the centre of force at all angles. Low aspect ratio rudders are likely to be heavy on the helm.

3   The planform area of the rudder often is related to the area of the lateral plane, 5 to 15 per cent being typical.

4   Skegged rudders improve the efficiency of the rudder when holding a course, but the skeg slows the rate of turning.

moved forward, the board turns away from the wind. It follows that there must be a position for the sail at which balance is achieved, all the forces being in perfect harmony as the board holds a straight course into the setting sun. Though, judging by the time many board sailors spend in the water rather than on their sailboards, this may take some imagination to visualize.

This kind of balance can be seen as the ideal for most sailing boats because the application of the rudder to hold the boat on course has a slowing effect. Since there is no opportunity to adjust the position of the sail plan while sailing as on a sailboard (except by changing sails), the designer must attempt to position the sail plan fore and aft so that good balance is achieved. So many boats have been designed that do not have good balance that knowing where to position the sail plan becomes an art form, and is one of the great mysteries of design.

Of greatest concern is that the boat should be balanced when sailing upwind. Imbalance on other points of sailing must be tolerated, though the way the sails are set and the boat is heeling will change the balance equation (*see* Fig 138).

If the boat turns into the wind when the tiller is released it is said to carry *weather helm*; if it has a tendency to turn away from the wind, the term applied is *lee helm*. Lee helm is undesirable because it can lead to a dangerous situation if the tiller is released, and because it increases the amount of leeway a boat makes, which detracts from the boat's windward performance. A small amount of weather helm usually meets with designers' and helmsmen's approval, though excesses are wearing and slow the boat.

Customary practice at the design stage is to consider the fore and aft position of the sail plan, as if sheeted on the centreline, relative to the lateral plane. Because it makes the task easier, the mainsail triangle (excluding roach), the foretriangle (excluding genoa overlap) and the basic triangle or quadrilateral of any other sails are used to find the *centroid* of the combined areas. The centroid is the centre of gravity of the combination, which can be found by cutting it out in card and balancing it on a straight edge (*see* Fig 139). Equally satisfactory results are obtained by geometrical construction from the sail plan (*see* Fig 140) or by taking moments of the areas.

Similarly, the centroid of the lateral plane (or underwater profile) is found most conveniently by balancing a piece of card the shape of

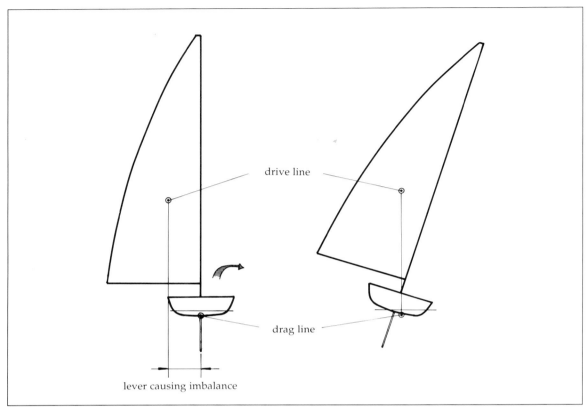

Fig 138   *The relative positions of drive and drag are critical to balance.*

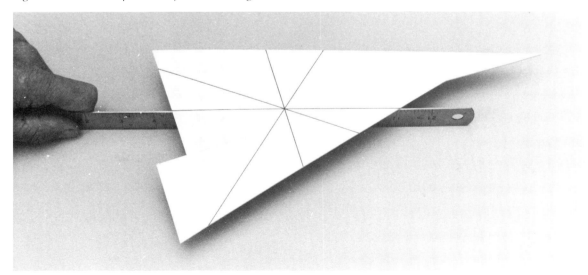

Fig 139   *Finding the centroid by balancing.*

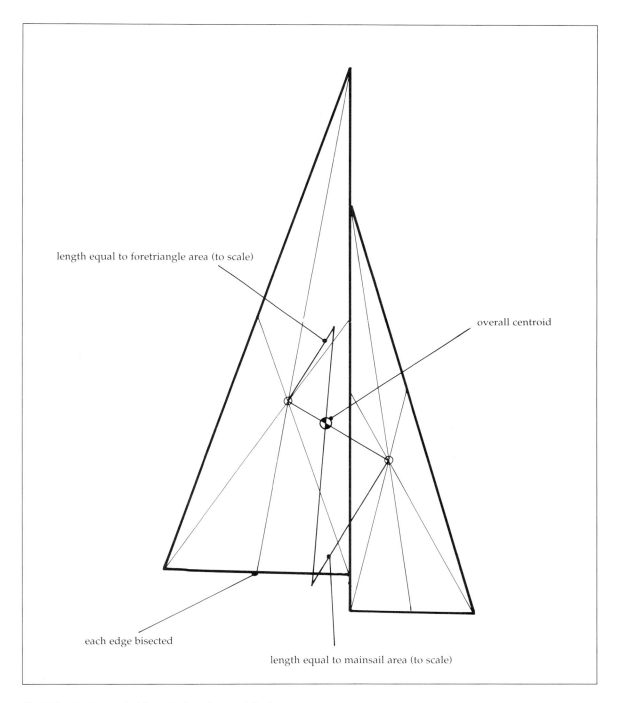

length equal to foretriangle area (to scale)

overall centroid

each edge bisected

length equal to mainsail area (to scale)

Fig 140   Or the centroid can be found geometrically.

Fig 141   A simple way of finding the centroid of the lateral plane.

the lateral plane (*see* Fig 141). Conventionally, the rudder is omitted.

It has been found that balance is achieved for most sailing craft when the centroid of the sail plan 'leads', that is, lies ahead of, the lateral plane centroid. This distance, termed the *lead*, could be 1m for a boat of 8m. In order to generalize, the distance usually is expressed as a percentage of the length water-line. Therefore, if our yacht of 8m has a water-line length of 7m, the lead as a percentage would be 14.3 per cent ($\frac{1}{7}$).

Experience has taught us that different types of boat require different values of lead. Unfortunately, there is a fair disagreement about what these values should be. I suggest the following: dinghies, 5 per cent; yachts, 10 per cent; ketches, 20 per cent; catamarans, 0 per cent, as a starting point only.

Although the use of lead is a textbook approach, some of its limitations spring instantly to mind. For example, a multihull's mainsail might or might not have a large roach, and it seems reasonable to account for whichever. Within the context of the method, two different leads could be devised for multihulls according to whether or not the roach is large. Allowance could also be made for features

outside the norm, such as large genoa overlap, long keel, deep forefoot and so on, but the method then becomes very complex.

Conventions do change and some designers prefer to base the sail centroid on the actual plan form of the sails and to include the rudder in the determination of the centroid of the lateral plane where the rudder is separate from the keel. Adopting this approach does produce different standard values for lead from those already presented.

Lead can be thought to be the factor that adapts the modelling of the situation to reality. An alternative example may help to explain how this works. Suppose the painter in a traditional boat-yard requires a simple way of finding the area of the topsides of boats so that the amount of paint needed can be judged. An accurate assessment could be made by taking a large number of measurements of the topsides, but since the throughput of boats to be painted is high, this kind of accuracy is unwarranted. He decides to measure the freeboard at its highest point and multiply this distance by the length overall, and then by two to account for both sides. Using this mathematical model, as it is described, he finds he needs more paint for some boat types and less for others as the model is not a perfect one.

Often, lead is treated rather like paint – there is a tendency to allow a bit extra 'to be on the safe side'. This occurred when a friend designed and built his own keelboat. Its construction demonstrated his philosophy of going up a size, so that its strength was guaranteed. But going up a size on the lead, to be sure it would not carry bad weather helm, resulted in – you've guessed it – bad lee helm. It was an awkward boat to sail.

The impression given is that there is an exact figure for the lead so that a boat will balance. This is a half truth – the balance is likely to be achieved in one wind strength only. It is common that when sailing to windward in a fresh breeze a yacht carries weather helm, and yet slight lee helm in a light breeze. Only between these two conditions is the yacht balanced.

There is an alternative philosophy, mainly belonging to the protagonists of yachts of double-ended form, where the stern shape is similar to the bow, and which also have a section not far from being circular. Such hulls present a little changed form to the water on heeling, the water-lines around the hull, in particular, remaining reasonably symmetrical fore and aft. It has been argued that the hull form is the key to balance and that forms so described are balanced intrinsically, irrespective of the positioning of the sail plan.

Without a doubt, the hull form affects balance. Modern craft of the full stern and fine bow genre do not continue in a straight line when heeled by ballasting, but turn away from the side towards which they are heeled (*see* Fig 142). But for all hull forms, the

Fig 142   The curved wake demonstrates the course that the model follows after a hefty shove.

SUMMARY — THE CONVENTIONAL APPROACH TO SAILING BALANCE

1   In order to produce balance – implying slight or zero weather helm – when sailing to windward, the centroid of the sail triangles should lead the centroid of the underwater profile, without rudder, by 0 to 20 per cent of the length water-line. Specific values are applied according to the sail plan and craft type.

2   For modern craft, an alternative approach is to determine the centroids based upon the sails' actual planform and the underwater profile inclusive of rudder, but this does imply modified standard values of lead.

3   Perfect balance may be achieved in one wind strength only. Some hull forms have better natural balance, less affected by heel.

---

positioning of the sail plan must affect the re-lationship of the forces acting and therefore the equilibrium, and a better understanding of balance can be gained by considering the forces of the wind in the sails and the water on the hull and appendages.

Forces and Sailing Balance

An immutable principle of science is that, within our everyday world, any system of forces must be in equilibrium, or otherwise move towards this state. Sometimes, equi-librium changes, as when we trip over, the out-of-balance forces being resolved finally when we are sprawled on the ground, equi-librium regained.

If the force on the sail plan of a yacht is out of balance with the force on the hull and keel combination, the rudder is applied to redress this (*see* Fig 143). If the rudder can supply in-sufficient force, the course cannot be main-tained and equilibrium is found at some point, perhaps when head to wind.

Although the centroid of the sail plan is often described for simplicity as the *centre of effort*, this is not technically correct. The centre of effort (or force) does not act at the centroid

when a boat sails to windward but forward of this point as a result of the aerodynamic force distribution (*see* Fig 144). For a sail, the centre of force lies approximately 35 per cent aft of the leading edge, depending upon the angle of attack, and slightly above the height of the centroid position.

For a sloop rig, the centre of effort can be predicted for each sail and then weighted ac-cording to the relative effectiveness of each (*see* Fig 145). The Davidson Laboratory has suggested a 63:37 weighting in favour of the jib. Thus every square metre of jib contributes 63 per cent and every square metre of mainsail 37 per cent of the total force produced by the sail plan.

A consideration of the mainsail and jib com-bination as a single aerofoil presents a simple, if incomplete, way of assessing the position of the centre of effort. One could suppose a posi-tion 35 per cent aft of the leading edge of the jib, though a figure rather less than this is likely.

The hydrodynamic force on the underwater surfaces comprising the hull and appendages must be equal and opposite to, and in line with, the aerodynamic force on the sails for equilibrium. Establishing the hydrodynamic centre of force is the more difficult because it

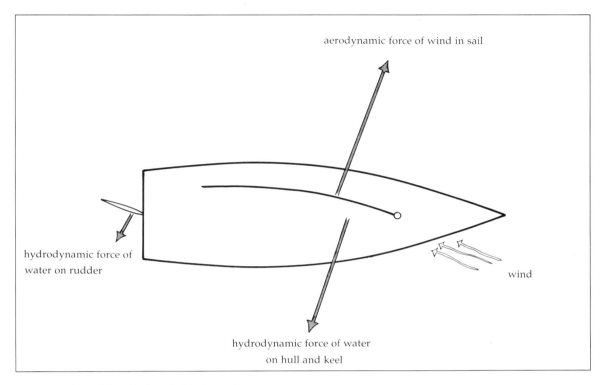

Fig 143   The rudder side force holds the yacht on course.

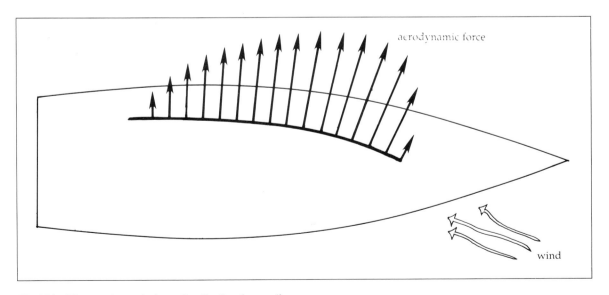

Fig 144   The aerodynamic force distribution for a sail.

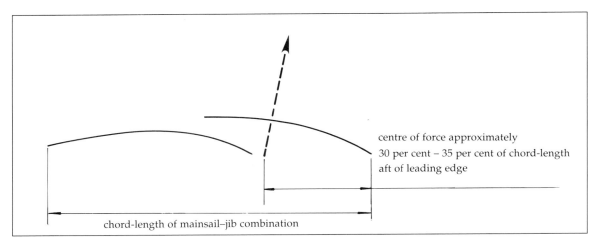

centre of force approximately
30 per cent – 35 per cent of chord-length
aft of leading edge

chord-length of mainsail–jib combination

Fig 145   The centre of force of the mainsail and jib combination.

is hard to predict the contribution made by the hull, which represents generally a rather poor foil. Nevertheless, the bow contributes significantly to the side force generated, not only because the underwater surface is reasonably close to being vertical, but because the centre of force of a foil lies close to the leading edge.

A stab at the overall hydrodynamic centre of force, known as the *centre of lateral resistance*, could be made by approximating separately the hull's and the keel's centres of force and then combining them by applying a weighting, as for the sail plan. The keel is a more effective surface for providing a side

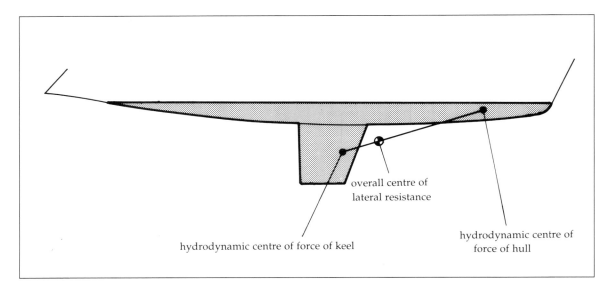

overall centre of
lateral resistance

hydrodynamic centre of force of keel

hydrodynamic centre of
force of hull

Fig 146   A consideration of the forces in finding the centre of lateral resistance.

force in comparison with the hull, on a plan-form area-for-area basis, and so the keel would be favoured. Fig 146 makes clearer the principle of this approach.

Judgement must be used in assessing the relative effectiveness of the hull, based upon how flat the bottom is. Greater exactitude is probably not called for. It has been found that some 3 degrees of helm shifts the centre of lateral resistance as much as 10 per cent of the length water-line, which implies a fair measure of tolerance.

Arguably, the rudder should be included in determining the centre of lateral resistance. If a boat is regarded as being well balanced when the helm is amidships, or with slight weather helm, it would be sensible for the rudder to figure in the analysis because the rudder does contribute towards resisting leeway.

A much simpler way of finding the centre of lateral resistance is by using a model of the boat towed at various positions until it requires no external correction to keep it on course. This does, of course, suppose that a model of the intended design is built.

In this way, proper account can be made for the effect of heel. The aerodynamic force is simulated by towing at the height of the centre of effort. Since the ratio of the driving force to side force of a sail plan when sailing to windward is about 1:3, the model should be towed at the angle this represents.

By adjusting the fore and aft position of the tow point, balance can be found for the simulated wind strength and angle of heel (*see* Fig 147). When balance is achieved, the aerodynamic force aligns with the hydrodynamic force (*see* Fig 148).

Unfortunately, the balance is specific to this angle of heel. If heel is increased, the aerodynamic force is further offset from the centreline and the forces no longer align. The consequence is that to keep the boat on course, it carries weather helm (*see* Fig 149). Similarly,

Fig 147(a)

Fig 147(b)

Fig 147(c)

Figs 147(a–c)   The model is towed from a position which simulates the aerodynamic centre of force. It is to be noted that the towing position must be further forward the greater the model is heeled, in order to maintain balance.

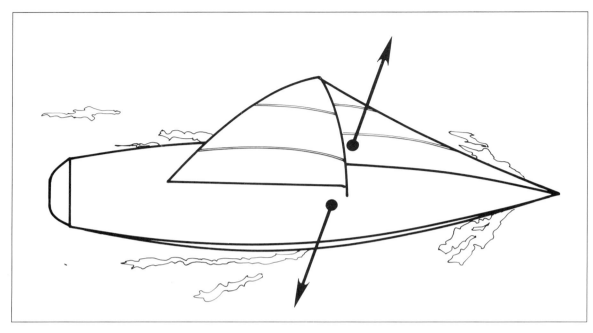

Fig 148   The aerodynamic and hydrodynamic forces balance.

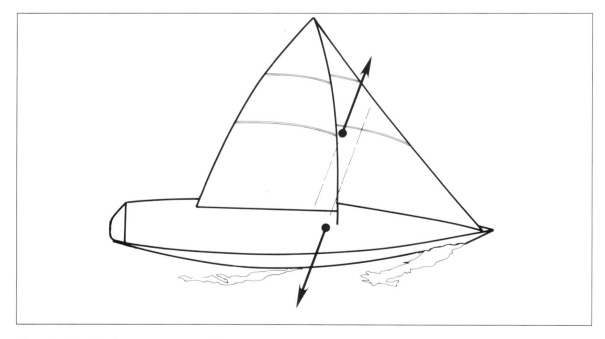

Fig 149   Out of balance, requiring weather helm to keep the yacht on course.

if the angle of heel is less than the angle at which balance occurs, the result is lee helm.

Achieving balance at all angles of heel, therefore, is seen to be unlikely, and the best one can target for is balance in moderate wind strengths and then tolerate a degree of weather helm or lee helm in other conditions. Because dinghies can both be heeled in light airs and yet held fairly upright in fresh conditions, balance can reasonably be maintained at all times.

Model testing of the kind described is not usually a practical proposition and so the positioning of the sail plan must rest upon judgement made on the drawing board. Although an attempt was made to predict the

true centres of effort and lateral resistance as an improvement over the use of centroids, allowance still must be made for angle of heel. Lead, therefore, still is required.

Just as for the conventional approach, lead will vary for different sailing craft types, though to a lesser degree. Specific allowance for high aspect ratio sail plans and long keels necessary for determining lead, using the principle of centroids, is taken care of when the true forces are considered. But hull form affects the issue. The very low or negative values of lead required for catamarans, resulting from the major shift of the *drag line*, provides an interesting example which makes this point (*see* Fig 150).

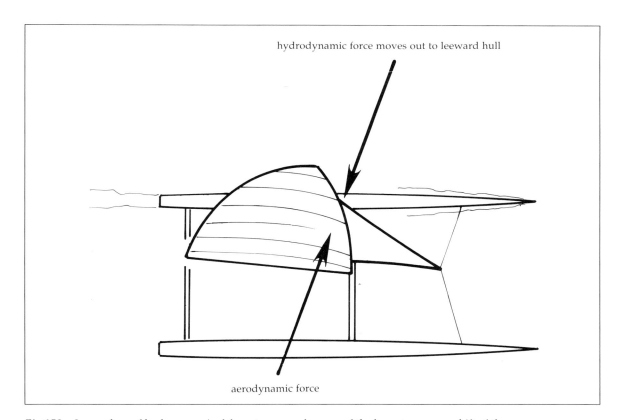

Fig 150   Low values of lead are required for catamarans because of the large transverse shift of the drag line.

SUMMARY — FORCES AND SAILING BALANCE

1   An improved system for modelling sailing craft balance seeks alignment of the aerodynamic and hydrodynamic forces.

2   The centre of effort of a single sail is about 35 per cent aft of the leading edge when sailing to windward, but, for sloop rigs, allowance needs to be made for the greater force produced by the jib. Similarly, the centre of lateral resistance is based upon the forces produced by keel, rudder and hull, proportioned according to their relative effectiveness.

3   Lead is required still so that the forces are aligned when heeled, and to allow for the tendency towards weather helm resulting from hull asymmetry.

Propeller Design

As a system for converting an engine's energy into propulsion, the propeller is one of the most efficient and convenient, and leaves standing the conventional paddle-wheel system used on shallow draught river steamers of old.

The basic principle underlying the propeller's operation is that a stream of water is accelerated astern, the reaction from which propels the boat forward. The relative movement of the propeller and the stream of water is achieved by the screw action of the propeller. Just like a wood screw, every turn produces a progression, in itself an important design criterion based upon water having the same unyielding qualities as wood.

This progression is termed the *pitch*. Because water is, in fact, yielding and there are losses as the water flows past the blades, the propeller does not produce a progression equal to the pitch but, depending upon its efficiency and the conditions prevailing, progresses a distance of 75–95 per cent of the pitch. This is known as the *advance*. The difference between the pitch and the advance is the *slip* (*see* Fig 151).

Propellers commonly have two, three or four blades. The use of just one blade is not practicable because the propeller would be unbalanced as it rotated. In accelerating water astern, each blade behaves as a foil, low pressure occurring on the *back* and high pressure on the *face*, the lift approximating to the thrust and the drag to the torsional force.

Reference to standard NACA sections reveals an interesting variety of possibilities. Since boats spend most of their time travelling forwards, the blades can be designed with an asymmetrical section, although this does reduce efficiency when going astern. This is like using an asymmetrical keel, which is better on one tack than on the other.

Very slow speed propellers work well with a section having a thickness to chord ratio of as much as 15 per cent, but as speed increases the water is shouldered aside by such a bluff section, and this prevents the water adhering to the blade. A blade's velocity towards the tip can be as high as 50m/s; the further from the hub, the greater is the velocity. Usually, the propeller's rotational velocity is a fraction (typically one-half or one-third) of the engine's rotational velocity, and this is achieved using a reduction gear.

With a typical velocity of 30–45m/s, the blades need to be reasonably thin, perhaps with a thickness to chord of 8 per cent for the lower velocity and 4 per cent for the higher, in

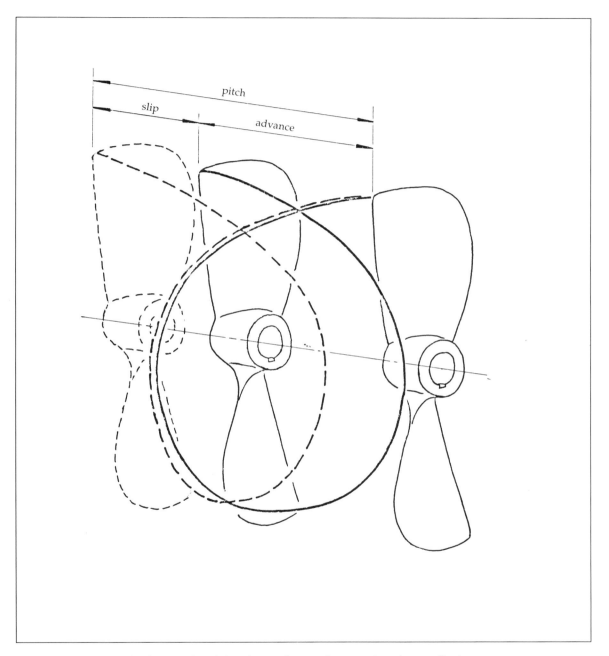

Fig 151   *The pitch is the theoretical, and the advance the actual progression of a propeller in one revolution.*

order for satisfactory flow to be maintained over the backs of the blades. If the flow breaks down because the blades are too thick or the leading edges too full, bubbles are formed and when they collapse the backs of the blades are eroded.

This process, known as *cavitation*, occurs because of the formation of very low pressure. At lowered pressures, water boils at a lower temperature. (It's difficult to make a good cup of tea when mountaineering because the water cannot be heated to a familiar 100°C. Conversely, the temperature to which water in a car's radiator system can be raised is higher when pressurized.) Thus, on the backs of the blades, the water literally boils.

Due to the problems associated with cavitation, not so very long ago there was a boat speed barrier of about 20m/s (40 knots). Although the limit speed is pushed upwards by the use of low propeller revolutions and large propeller diameter, the latter represents a physical handicap. Operating at the cavitation threshold is also undesirable because of potentially severe erosion damage to the blades.

The alternative is to design the blades deliberately to cavitate. This requires a sharp-edged section which knifes into the water producing a vapour cavity on the backs of the blades. Such sections are termed *fully cavitating* and achieve higher lift–drag ratios under these conditions.

Care must be taken in the design of the face of fully cavitating sections because this largely determines the shape of the cavity. Provided the back does not interfere with the cavity, its shape is irrelevant, sometimes a wedge section being chosen to provide maximum strength in a relatively thin section (*see* Fig 152). These often are called *cleaver* propellers.

The plan form of such propellers is usually as shown in Fig 153. Their mode of operation is somewhat brutal since they grab lumps of water and throw them backwards at great speed. In fact, with some systems of drive in which the drive shaft emerges from the transom, the propeller is surface piercing, and with some types fully half the number of blades are out of the water at any one time. The design of such propellers for high-speed work is in part empirical because it is hard to analyze the water flow round a propeller turning at the speeds required, especially as it is half in and half out of the water.

High-speed craft usually employ a stern drive system, either of the type described above or where the drive is taken through two right angles to place the propeller on a leg

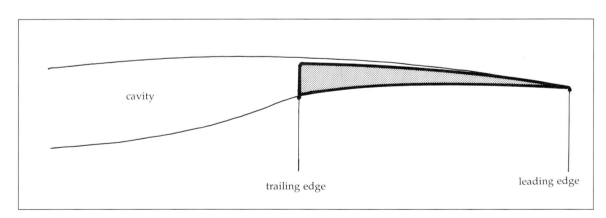

Fig 152   A fully cavitating section.

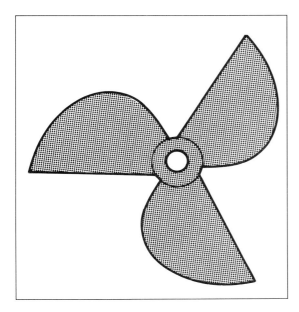

Fig 153   *The planform of a propeller used for high-speed craft.*

Fig 154   *A bow thruster. A transverse tube is built in to the bow area and the propeller is mounted within it.*

beneath the hull. The advantages of these systems include the horizontal drive line which can be achieved, and the beneficial effect at high speed of being able to place the engine well aft.

More conventional drive systems in which the propeller shaft emerges from the hull and is supported by a bracket, have the advantage of being tried and tested, but the disadvantages of a steep shaft angle and high drag around the bracketry supporting the propeller shaft. Usually two propellers are fitted, each well away from the centreline in order to minimize draught problems.

Designers of displacement craft often decide to run the shaft through the keel, which serves to protect the propeller. Greatest efficiency comes from tapering the keel and designing the stern so that water will flow readily to the propeller. Eddies in the water disrupt the flow and this can cause cavitation. Tapering the keel also minimizes the pulse,

which occurs when each blade passes the keel. This 'dead zone' also initiates cavitation and the shaft likes it not a bit because of the momentary bending and torsional loads imposed.

Sailing craft present a different requirement which results from a need for an engine and propeller only occasionally. For the majority of the time, the propeller is as useful as a spare tyre around a marathon runner's midriff. The propeller drag while sailing can be minimized by locating the propeller in an area where eddies already occur, such as behind the ballast keel or in an aperture in the skeg or keel deadwood.

Performance sailing yachts often use *folding* or *feathering* propellers (*see* Fig 155) in order to minimize drag when sailing, though their efficiency under power is less than a conven-

Fig 155(a)   The blades of a folding propeller
automatically close for least drag when sailing.

Fig 155(b)   Under power, the propeller blades
open due to centrifugal force.

Fig 156(a)   More drag results when the
propeller rotates . . .

Fig 156(b)   . . . than when it is fixed.

tional propeller. Performance when going astern can be uncertain, the folding propeller relying upon centrifugal force to hold the blades in position.

It is usual to use two blades only for sailing yachts' propellers, whether they are of folding, feathering or solid-bladed pattern. The drag of each propeller installation can be compared. For a sample propeller of 0.5m (1.5ft) diameter and with the boat travelling at 3m/s (6 knots), the following drag figures would be typical: 200N (45lb) for an exposed shaft installation with a solid-bladed propeller; 50N (10lb) for a feathering propeller; 30N (7lb) for a folding propeller.

When it is considered that the total resistance of a 9m (30ft) sailing yacht at this speed is likely to be about 500N (110lb), the proportionate drag is seen to be significant, if not huge. However, at 3m/s (6 knots) the yacht would be close to maximum displacement speed, and the slowing effect of a propeller would not be as alarming as may appear, though the reduction in speed may be in the order of 8, 1½, and 1 per cent respectively for each propeller installation example. At maximum displacement speed, little effect on speed would be noticed whatever type of propeller were carried, because the hull's resistance is itself so high, but at low speeds the drop in speed is marked.

It is rare that three-bladed propellers are carried, though large heavy-displacement cruising yachts and motor sailers may well be able to tolerate the drag when sailing presented by a behemoth three-bladed solid propeller. The reader gets full marks for thinking that drag can be reduced by allowing the propeller to rotate freely in the water. Unfortunately, unless the propeller is extremely free moving, tests show that drag is higher when allowed to rotate (*see* Fig 156).

SUMMARY — PROPELLER DESIGN

1   The blades of a screw propeller behave as foils, experiencing low pressure on the backs and high pressure on the faces. Conventional sections are suitable at low blade speeds.

2   At the high blade velocities required for high-speed craft, the back pressure reduces to such an extent that the water cavitates. Thin, cleaver-type sections are called for.

3   The propeller can be protected by the propeller shaft running through a keel, but it should be tapered in order to minimize eddies.

4   For sailing yachts, low-drag propellers often are used. Solid-bladed propellers usually produce least drag when prevented from rotating.

Chapter 5

About the Lines Plan

Drawing the Lines

Up until about a hundred years ago, the major part of the yacht designer's occupation was spent whittling away at a block of wood in his lap, no doubt taking great care that his knife did not slip. The personal hazards for his successors are less dramatic. Working over a drawing board leads only to dentist's spine and jeweller's squint, while computer whizz-kid designers get goggle-eyed from glaring at the screen too much.

The whittler shaped his block of wood to produce a half-model of the intended shape (*see* Fig 157), the process being a highly visual one which tested the designer's appreciation for a satisfying shape and a fair line. From the measurements of the finished half-model, the yacht would be built. These measurements were obtained most easily by sawing the half-model into a series of slabs or planks, or alternatively by dowelling together a number of planks, shaping the model and then separating the planks.

Perhaps a minor fault of this system of design was that sometimes adjustments would have to be made to the frames when building because the wooden planking which skins the frames would not follow naturally the curvature of the hull. However, a good designer/builder would develop an eye for what could and could not be done.

The method is a satisfying one and has not lost relevance today; indeed, since relatively few boats are now planked, there is little re-

Fig 157   A half-model built from layers of wood.

striction on shape from a constructional point of view. However, the modern version of model building is by constructing wire frames on the computer screen where, it has to be said, slices of the hull can be put back much more easily than on the physical model.

It was felt, around 80 BC (Before Computers), that the system of design using half-models was lacking the application of science. For instance, the calculation of displacement, which is significant in that it positions the water-line, was not generally applied in the half-model era. There also was a resistance to more modern, scientific approaches. One of the first boats designed initially on the drawing board (*Vindex* in 1870) received much scorn and was dubbed ungraciously a 'paper boat' by the whittlers.

The principle of designing the hull on a flat

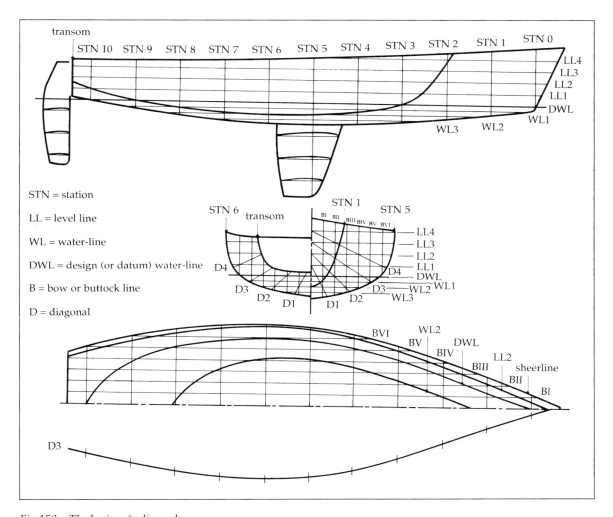

Fig 158   The basics of a lines plan.

surface rests upon representing the three-dimensional form in two dimensions. This approach has been used for more than a century and is not without its supporters, even in this silicon chip era. The form in which the lines plan is drawn has changed little, though draughting film is the preferred medium rather than paper or cloth, because film is far more stable in changing conditions of humidity.

Fig 158 shows an example of a lines plan but with sample lines only for demonstration purposes. The following description should be read in conjunction with the lines plan.

Just like the half-model, the lines plan represents one-half of the hull only, on the basis that it is symmetrical about its centreline. If a half-model is sawn (using a very fine saw blade) into a series of equal-thickness slabs and the outline of each slab is drawn on paper

135

(or film), we basically have all the information required to identify the hull shape. There is, in fact, one small piece of additional information required, and this is the thickness of the slabs.

If the slabs are cut horizontally, the outlines they produce are termed *water-lines*. Purists would say that they should be referred to as water-lines when below the design water-line, which is the water-line at which the boat is expected to float, and *level lines* above it. The water-lines and level lines do provide enough information for the frames to be constructed at full size and the boat built.

However, in order that the designer can visualize the hull form from different directions, a number of sets of cutting planes is used. Because the hull form is defined by any one set of cutting planes, an excess of information is provided by the lines plan, but this serves as a check.

Conventionally, the cutting planes used are the *water-lines* and *level lines* already described, the *sections* which are vertical and perpendicular to the centreline, the *bow and buttock lines* which are vertical and parallel to the centreline plane, the bow lines being forward of amidships and the buttock lines aft, and the *diagonals*. A diagonal represents the outline of a cutting plane made at an angle to the centreline plane. Usually, a series of diagonals is drawn through a range of angles.

For many hull forms, the diagonals are the most important of the lines. The designer intends that each of the diagonals should cross the sections approximately at right angles, though as any one diagonal runs forward and aft it is unlikely to intersect all the sections in this manner. Not only do the diagonals define the hull more accurately than any other lines, but they most closely resemble the path which water takes in flowing around the hull. The diagonals, therefore, can be used to ensure that neither abrupt changes nor severe curvature are present.

When drawing a lines plan by hand, the fore

and aft lines – diagonals, water-lines and level lines, and bow and buttock lines – are drawn using a *batten*, basically to guide the drawing pen or pencil. Battens are normally made from flexible plastic of small cross-section. They are available either of parallel or tapered section, tapered battens being used where more curvature at one end of the line is required, as in the case of a sheerline.

The value in using battens to draw lines is that they tend to produce *fair* lines. A fair curve is one around which the water should flow easily. The batten also simulates at small scale the curvature which would be adopted by a fore and aft plank. Setting up the batten so that a fair line can be drawn is a process with the same mystique that surrounds the

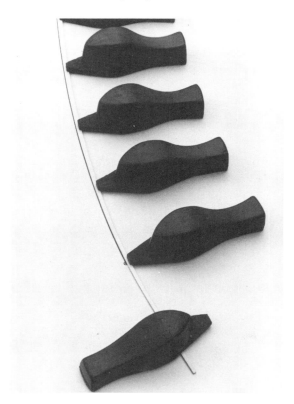

Fig 159   A tapered batten with spring. The weights are purpose made.

carving of half-models by eye. Weights are used to hold the batten to shape. It is important to weight the batten beyond the line to be drawn, and often to give the batten some *spring* at the ends to avoid a flattening of the line (*see* Fig 159). A minimum of weights should be used to hold the batten, since this is likely to produce the most fair line. To make a final check on fairness, each weight in turn is removed and then replaced, the batten not moving if the line is fair. Of course, the end two weights are not removed as this would cause the batten to spring free, thereby disturbing the whole batten.

Where the curvature is too severe for a batten, *curves* are used as a drawing template (*see* Fig 160). It is rare that a curve will match ex-actly the complete line to be drawn, in which case the line is drawn in parts, a section of a curve being found which does match exactly the part. Typically, and for a reasonably small lines plan, curves would be used for the drawing of the sections. Different families of curves are available to suit different purposes, but usually the shapes have a curve which is gentle and becomes more severe in a progressive manner.

The way in which the lines plan is developed varies with personal preference and the shape of the hull. The first stage is always the drawing of a grid to represent the straight 'edges' of all the cutting planes. A profile of the hull may be drawn next, forming the outline of the *profile plan*. A bird's-eye view of the

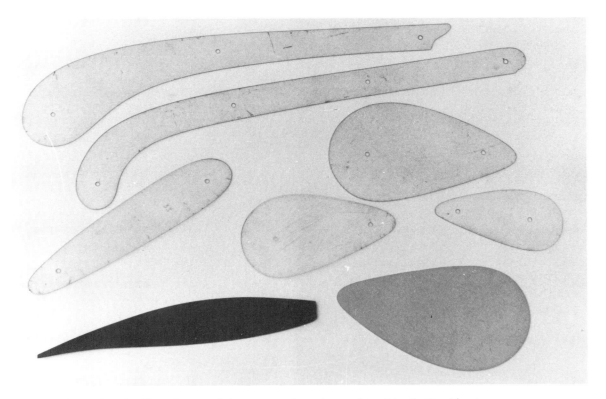

Fig 160 A selection of well-used curves. It is easy to make one's own from thin plastic, either to a standard shape or to choice, as shown by the two curves in the foreground.

SUMMARY – DRAWING THE LINES

1   During the last century, designers favoured shaping a half-model to develop the shape of the hull. This method has been superseded by drawing a lines plan.

2   Cutting planes are used to represent the hull form, these being horizontal, vertical in both transverse and longitudinal planes, and at an angle to the centreline approximately perpendicular to the sections.

3   The lines are drawn using either a batten held down by weights or otherwise curves are used to guide the drawing pen or pencil.

4   For simplicity of calculation, the length water-line may be split into eleven stations, but a spacing to suit the frame positions may be preferred by the builder.

deck might follow, to form the basis of the *half-breadth plan*. Then some sections might be sketched to form the basis of the *body plan*. These sections provide guide points for the drawing of the diagonals, water-lines and level lines and bow and buttock lines. The order in which these groups of lines are drawn depends upon the hull form, though it is unlikely that one would complete one group to the neglect of the other two. The sections would then be drawn accurately based upon the lines already drawn. Of fundamental importance is that the lines should correspond in all three views.

It makes sense to space the water-lines equidistantly, as it does for the level lines, bow and buttock lines and sections. This helps the fairing and the visualization of the shape, rather as the gradient is indicated by the contours of an ordnance survey map. This is particularly true for the sections, which give the best impression of the shape of the hull form.

The sections are located at positions termed *stations*. Conventionally, the design water-line is split into eleven stations in order to make the calculations for the hull as simple as possible. This usually means that the station spacing is one of those nasty lengths with lots of

digits after the decimal point. The designer may be cursed for this by the boat builder who must draw the lines plan at boat size (called *lofting*) to ensure accuracy, and funny numbers can lead to unfunny mistakes and even less funny remarks.

The builder may wish also to use a greater or lesser spacing for the setting up of the frames and this leads to more work. The alternative is to space the stations using a nice wholesome distance such as one metre, and then worry about the calculations later. Given a good understanding of the principles, and a little help from electronic wizardry, this presents few major problems.

Lines by Computer

As a glorified calculator, the computer's number-crunching capability has been seized upon by many designers for routine calculations as a real time saver, but the adaptation of graphics software from other industries for drawing hull lines moves boat design work into another dimension. Computer-aided design (CAD) really does take two-dimensional lines-plan work into three dimensions.

Although computer graphics can create 'virtual reality', it is too easy for 'users' to panegyrize the deity every time they 'boot up'. Computers and software are best treated with an element of suspicion and perhaps irreverence. Programs are based upon mathematical models of reality, and it is hard to know what assumptions or approximations the programmer has made.

For example, a program might offer to provide a resistance prediction for a range of boats. The program could well be 'user-friendly' and trot out its prediction, perhaps with an impressive graph. However, it is unlikely to make clear the process or mathematical model used in coming to its (strictly, the programmer's) predictions.

At one extreme, an intricate analysis could be made of the expected behaviour of the water as it flows around the defined hull form, in order to produce a prediction of resistance. Then again, resistance could be determined by a crude formula based only upon displacement, which takes no real account of the shape of the hull (for example, a formula which assumes resistance to be equal to 3.5–4 per cent of a boat's displacement at maximum displacement speed). The problem is that we are unlikely to know the quality of the prediction without knowledge of the mathematical modelling used.

While I am feeling irreverent, perhaps I should say that in CAD terms there is nothing special about boats. A shoe could be designed on the screen using the same techniques as are used to design boats. This is not to say that your size nine's displacement would be calculated, only that they both are fairly simple three-dimensional forms.

A number of specific or *dedicated* programs for drawing hull lines are available. Some provide the user with a basic shape to start with. It doesn't matter if this shape looks like a short length of guttering or like a six-year-old's cardboard model of Daddy's new boat.

The basic shape appears as a series of representational lines as for a lines plan; or a *wire frame* can be conjured, and can be rotated so that you can see what a gutter or Daddy's new boat looks like from different angles. Using a *mouse*, which translates movement of the hand into movement on the screen, or by using the keyboard, you can pull the lines in or out, up or down, until they close on your dream (or dreamy) design.

Once the basic shape is established, further lines can be added in order better to define the shape. It helps to think of the surface as a rubber sheet which can be distorted at will. The lines are faired (or *smoothed* in computer jargon) automatically by the computer.

Alternatively, the hull form might be started by inputting, via a mouse, the basic shape intended, based on a stern section, midship section and bow profile. Points on these *master curves* would then be joined by fair lines to give the framework of a lines plan. Or, instead of playing with mice one can input the points by keying in the co-ordinates, as in Fig 161 which shows a master section. The real work of modification then begins.

All this takes time, perhaps as much time as is required to draw a lines plan conventionally. One bonus in using a CAD system for the lines plan work is the rotatable wire frame feature, but for a designer familiar with his medium this quasi-three-dimensional representation may be overrated. But they do look nice, except at some angles when wire frames don't look quite right. What you see is not always what you get.

The smoothing function can be unpredictable until one is familiar with the way the points influence the smoothed line. Sometimes it happens that one wishes to fix a measurement point or section of the boat, and this can be a little difficult. Sophisticated designs require sophisticated CAD skills.

In the lines plan drawing contest of draughtsperson versus machine, each opponent

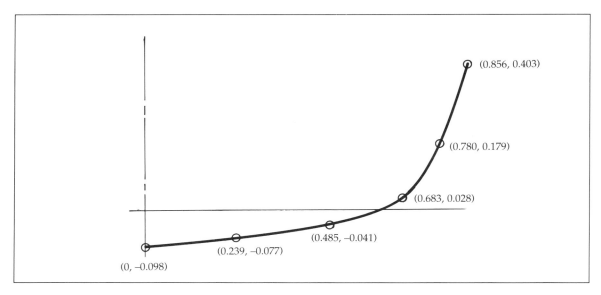

Fig 161   Co-ordinates which establish a master curve.

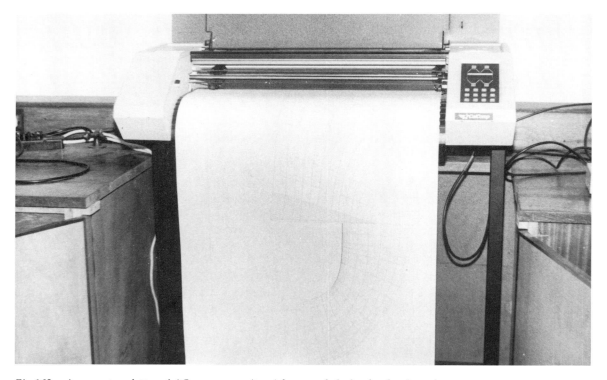

Fig 162   A computer plotter of AO paper capacity. A large-scale body plan has been drawn.

so far is well matched with one round apiece, perhaps with CAD showing a slight lead on points because it is faster for preliminary design work. But in the following rounds, CAD draws well ahead.

For conventional lines-plan work, measurements (termed *offsets*), of points along all the lines are expressed on an offset table which is used to draw out the lines plan at full size. The lofting of the lines plan enables the frames to be built. With a CAD system, press the right button and the offsets are printed before you can say 'random access memory'. Two rounds to one.

The lines can be drawn to the scale required using a *plotter*, which draws with pens to an accuracy of something like one-tenth of a millimetre (*see* Figs 162–163). Plotting the lines plan is not a necessity, but may reassure the boat

builder who is likely to be familiar with this format. In fact, it only is necessary to send him the offsets, either printed out or on a floppy disc, which is a piece of plastic on which information can be stored. Such is the potential of the software's fairing capability, with offsets presented to a one-millimetre accuracy, that lofting is not necessary. CAD three, draughtsperson one.

An alternative to presenting the boat builder with the offsets is to send him the sections required for the frames. These can be plotted at full size on film. Four rounds to one. Unfortunately, plotters of this ilk, and for that matter all the equipment that goes with them, cost megabucks, which pulls back a round for the lines-plan-by-hand, offsets and lofting approach. Low-priced hardware with a cheap and cheerless monitor (or visual display unit – VDU)

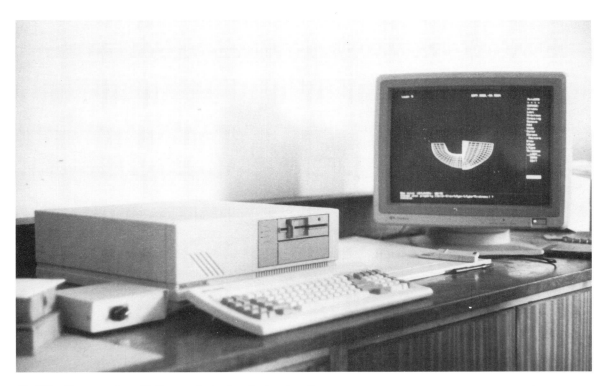

Fig 163   The computer with the same body plan displayed on the screen.

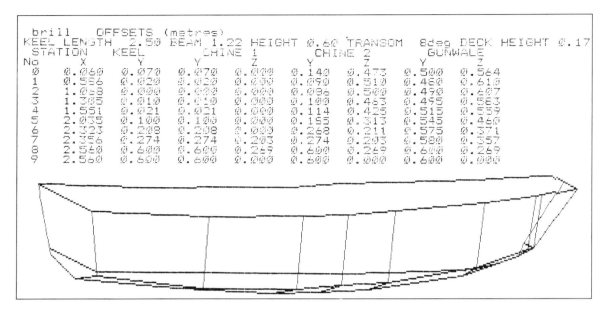

Fig 164   Offsets and printout of a small rowing dinghy designed by one of my students, using low-cost hardware.

Fig 165   The dinghy in the flesh – or in the aluminium, strictly speaking!

and a printer rather than plotter, produces the kind of result shown in Figs 164 and 165. Fig 166 shows a plotted wire frame for comparison.

Given a *numerically controlled* machine-tool facility (a system for machining shapes based on computer offsets), the frames could be cut out at full size, and keels and rudders could be machined directly. Panels for the hull skin could be cut to the shape prescribed by the offsets. This use of computer-aided manufacture (CAM) has much to offer boat building, though relatively low-volume production in most boat-yards and high investment costs do militate against this approach.

For the designer, the most significant offering made by CAD is that all the calculations based on the hull generated on the screen are completed. This saves the designer having to work through these calculations, and any changes made to the hull result in an immediate updating of the calculations. It's a knockout.

All the calculations in the sections following (and more) are completed in an unbelievably small fraction of the time required manually or using a calculator. The reader might wonder whether or not it is necessary to know how to do these calculations when a CAD system creates the whole package. In my view, it is necessary in order to enhance one's

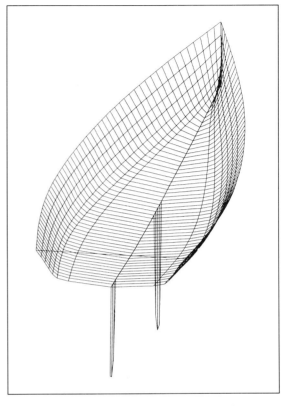

Fig 166   Plotters produce high-quality lines quickly. This plot was produced in less than half a minute.

SUMMARY — LINES BY COMPUTER

1   Computer-aided design offers the capability for representing the lines plan as a three-dimensional form. Rotatable wire-frame perspectives assist visualization.

2   Lines can be pulled, distorted and supplemented via a mouse or by inputting co-ordinates, and they can be smoothed.

3   Significant advantages lie in the constant updating and instant accessibility of offsets and hull-form calculations. Sections can be plotted at full size.

4 Linked to a computer-aided manufacture facility, keels and other components can be machined directly.

understanding and so that one can question the approach or mathematical model utilized. And who knows, one day every computer could be hit by a global, terminal virus.

Flotation of the Hull

Boats float. Everyone knows that. Everyone did not know that in the early 1800s when iron was first used for ship construction. It was reasoned (by the public at large, I hasten to add, rather than by members of the naval architecture profession) that, because iron sinks in water, ships built from this material would do likewise. We now know that hollowing a gargantuan piece of metal gives sufficient buoyancy to keep it afloat.

The principle of flotation rests upon water pressure, which increases with depth and results in a force on the hull which can be represented by a series of vectors (arrows indicating the forces), as in Fig 167. Each vector has a vertical component and the sum of these supports the boat in the water.

Although I make something of a leap in reasoning and express myself with some lack of rigour, each vertical component produces a force equal to the weight of a column of water from the hull bottom to the water-line. There-fore, the sum of these components, the *upthrust*, is equal to the weight of all the columns of water, that is, the weight of all the water which would occupy the hull (of negligible skin thickness) up to its water-line. Alternatively, we can think of the upthrust being equal to the weight of the water displaced by the hull when in water.

It was Archimedes, the Greek philosopher and mathematician, who first made clear this principle. It struck him so powerfully while taking advantage of the local municipal baths (the water got out when he got in) that he is said to have leapt from the baths and run naked through the streets shouting 'Eureka', meaning 'I have found it', i.e. that the upthrust on a body, in this case his own, is equal to the weight of water displaced. His interest was not, in fact, in naval architecture but in finding a way of assaying gold.

As far as objects which float are concerned, including boats, the weight must be equal to the upthrust. Therefore, a boat's weight must be equal to the weight of all the water displaced by the boat.

If all this seems like a load of flotsam, then try a more experimental bath-time approach. Locate a model hull, constructed ideally in fibreglass, and weigh it on the kitchen or bathroom scales. If you can't locate a model, use a

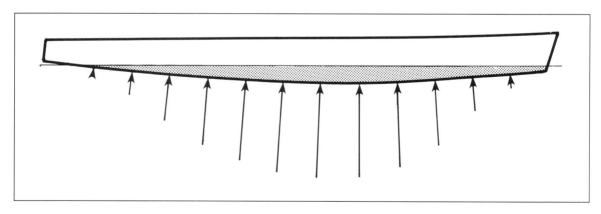

Fig 167   The forces resulting from water pressure on the hull.

SUMMARY — FLOTATION OF THE HULL

1   The hull is enabled to float by the vertical components of the forces of water pressure on the underwater part of the hull.

2   The weight of the boat is equal to the weight of water displaced by the hull. This has the same volume as the water which would fill the hull, assuming negligible skin thickness, to its water-line.

---

container such as a plastic bowl or sandwich box. Float the 'hull' in the bathwater and mark the water-line in a few places. Transfer these marks to the inside of the hull with the help of a strong light shone from the outside. Fill the hull with water to this line. Now weigh the hull plus water, whereupon it should be found (by subtraction) that the weight of the

water is approximately the same as the weight of the hull.

A more sophisticated experiment involves the use of a 'eureka can' so beloved by science teachers for verifying Archimedes' principle (*see* Fig 168). Otherwise, be inventive with plastic ducks and toy tugs in the bath, but be sure to don at least a towel when the penny drops and you wish to broadcast your discovery to the neighbours!

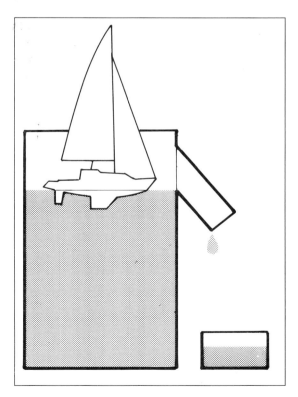

Fig 168   Archimedes rules OK.

Agreement of Mass and Displacement

So Archimedes tells us that the weight of the displaced water must equal the boat's weight. It follows that the mass of this water, the boat's *displacement*, must equal the mass of the boat.

This is of importance at the design stage because it is necessary to calculate the mass of the volume of water up to the water-line derived from the lines plan, and ensure that it agrees with the predicted mass of the boat obtained by summing the expected masses of all parts of the boat. Often it does not, in which case remedial action must be taken, although a close rather than an exact agreement is sought.

Unfortunately, things get tougher still. Not only must there be a correspondence between the mass and the displacement, but the centre of gravity of the mass and the centre of displacement, known as the *centre of buoyancy,* must align. In other words, the centre of gravity must be vertically above, below or coincident with the centre of buoyancy. This puts more balls into the air to juggle.

A major mistake is to complete the lines plan without consideration of the boat's mass and its centre of gravity. For example, if the mass were too high for the volume of displacement, unwanted transom drag could result from the boat's floating lower than expected. Also, the reduction in freeboard might be detrimental to seaworthiness.

Alternatively, to design the construction so that the boat must be more or less heavily built or ballasted, in order that it will float to its waterline, clearly is unsatisfactory, if not unsafe. The best approach to adopt is that of working on a preliminary lines plan and mass estimate before moving on to the final drawing and calculations. Even so, some boats are ballasted to bring them down to their marks, the ballast being placed as low as possible.

The mass calculation is probably the most tedious part of boat design work. Items such as winches, cookers, toilets and life-rafts often have their masses indicated on manufacturers' catalogues, or can be obtained directly from the manufacturers, but the mass of the hull skin, frames, reinforcement and so on can only be determined from the dimensions and the densities of the materials used. The final mass calculation may well comprise several hundred items. A preliminary mass estimate could be made on the basis of ten or twenty main items, a number of minor items being considered as one.

Generally, once the preliminary mass calculation is completed, the displacement and hence the underwater volume can be gauged. Since the displacement is equal to the mass of the volume of water, we can find the displacement from knowing the density of the water in which we expect the boat to be floating. The density of sea water is approximately 1025kg/m^3. Density increases with salinity and other dissolved salts but reduces with rising temperature. Fresh water (at *standard temperature*) has a density of 1000kg/m^3.

Thus, if the volume to a particular waterline, known as the *volume of displacement*, is 3m^3, the displacement would be 3000kg for fresh water and 3075kg for sea water. In general, the displacement is the product of the volume of displacement and the density of the water in which the boat is expected to float.

Mass and Centre of Gravity Calculations

Thus, the mass calculation is undertaken at two levels, one preliminary, one final, as the design progresses. In each case the process is the same, varying only in the level of tedium,

---

SUMMARY — AGREEMENT OF MASS AND DISPLACEMENT

1   There must be agreement between the boat's displacement (the product of the volume of displacement and the density of the water in which the boat is expected to float) and its mass (the sum of the masses of all its component parts).

2   The centres of buoyancy (of displacement) and gravity (of mass) must align vertically.

3   At the preliminary design stage, the above values are estimated using limited information, but at the final stage in the design a better agreement is sought from more accurate, detailed calculations.

---

and of course one's tolerance or liking for number crunching. For a task like this, the human brain betters the computer in many respects. (Computers are at their finest when required for repetitive calculations rather than intelligent guesswork and, of course, have a bit of an edge when it comes to speed.)

Judgement often is needed in making approximations, for instance in deciding to omit the mass of an item on the grounds that its effect will be negligible. We do not need the mass calculated to the nearest gram (nor kilogram most probably), nor the centre of gravity established to the nearest millimetre, and we are good at knocking a bit off here and adding a bit there to give a good estimate.

In addition to the total mass, it is necessary to determine the overall centre of gravity both longitudinally and vertically. The longitudinal centre of gravity (LCG) is required to check alignment with the longitudinal centre of buoyancy (LCB), while the vertical centre of gravity (VCG) provides an important indicator of stability.

Both LCG and VCG are determined by taking *moments* of the individual masses of the boat's components. (Strictly speaking, moments should be a function of weight rather than mass.) The moment of each of the components is assessed by the product of its mass and its perpendicular distance from a point. Two points are established, one for LCG and the other for VCG.

This is best explained by example. The point about which moments are taken can be anywhere, but for convenience the bow is chosen in order to find LCG. At one time, a point on the midships section was usually favoured so that moments generally were smaller. For example, the moment of an aft winch is less from amidships than from the bow. When slide rules were the norm for tackling such work and particularly when performing calculations for ships where binoculars have to be used to see the other end, this may have had merit, but with the advent of the calculator and computer there is no advantage in taking moments from amidships rather than from one end of the boat.

VCG is established from any point on the base line, which could be the DWL, but it simplifies the calculation to choose a line outside any of the masses, such as the bottom of the keel, the vertical height of all masses above this line being measured.

It is convenient to tabulate the mass, LCG and VCG calculations, but it should be realized that LCG and VCG are separate calculations. The final calculation of LCG is the sum of the moments from the base line divided by the sum of the masses, and similarly for VCG. The final centre of gravity position lies horizontally and vertically from the respective points.

An example is provided. The table, Fig 169, relates to the masses and their locations shown in the yacht in Fig 170.

For those readers eager for more, I include a computer program written in BASIC (*see* Fig 171). This is suitable for the most humble of

---

SUMMARY — MASS AND CENTRE OF GRAVITY CALCULATIONS

1   The final mass and centre of gravity calculations are based upon the individual masses and longitudinal and vertical centre of gravity positions from suitable data.

2   The overall centre of gravity of the boat from each datum is given by the sum of the moments from the datum divided by the sum of the masses (the total mass).

Item	A Mass (kg)	B Horizontal distance aft of bow (m)	A × B Horizontal moment (kg m)	C Vertical distance above keel base line (m)	A × C Vertical moment (kg m)
Anchor + warp	15	0.6	9	2.0	30
Rig	50	3.0	150	7.2	360
Interior	150	3.4	510	1.4	210
Keel	750	3.6	2700	0.6	450
Hull	300	4.1	1230	1.6	480
Deck + coachroof + cockpit	250	4.3	1075	2.1	525
Engine	150	4.8	720	1.4	210
Rudder	25	7.0	175	1.0	25
Sum of masses = 1690		Sum of horizontal moments = 6569		Sum of vertical moments = 2290	

Total mass = 1690kg

$$\text{LCG} = \frac{\text{sum of horizontal moments}}{\text{sum of masses}} = \frac{6569}{1690} = \textbf{3.89m aft of bow}$$

$$\text{VCG} = \frac{\text{sum of vertical moments}}{\text{sum of masses}} = \frac{2290}{1690} = \textbf{1.36m above keel}$$

Fig 169   Mass, LCG and VCG calculation.

machines, such as a pocket computer (see Fig 172), although memory presents a difficulty which limits the number of items that can be input. The number of items and the mass, LCG and VCG of each item in turn must be input. The vessel's overall mass, LCG and VCG are displayed.

Estimates of Displacement

Since the displacement of a boat is determined by the simple process of multiplying the volume of displacement by the water density, the real task is resolved into determining the volume of displacement. This can be approached at two levels, firstly to provide a preliminary estimate (or 'guesstimate') accurate to within 5 or 10 per cent, and secondly an estimate to an accuracy within about 2 per cent.

The advantage of the preliminary estimate is that it can be accomplished quickly. One approach is to make a judgement about the design's likely prismatic coefficient. For a yacht with fine ends relative to the middle body, the prismatic coefficient is about 0.50, average yacht forms figure at about 0.54, and a powered craft with an immersed transom stern would have a prismatic coefficient of some 0.65.

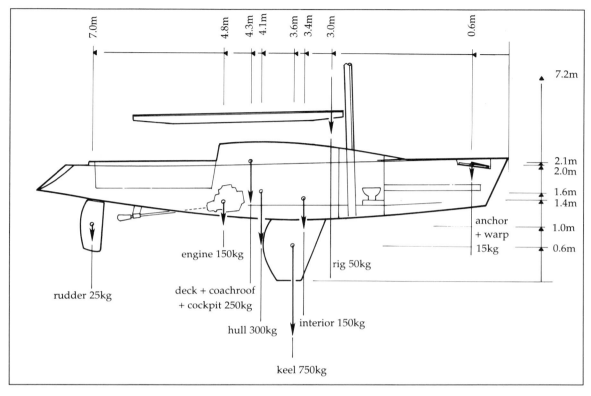

Fig 170   The masses and centre of gravity locations of the components of a small yacht.

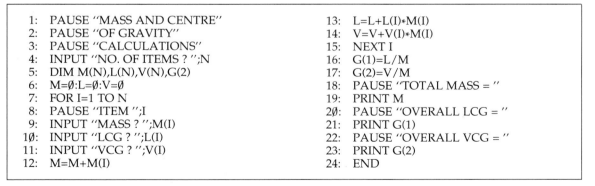

```
 1:   PAUSE "MASS AND CENTRE"          13:   L=L+L(I)*M(I)
 2:   PAUSE "OF GRAVITY"               14:   V=V+V(I)*M(I)
 3:   PAUSE "CALCULATIONS"             15:   NEXT I
 4:   INPUT "NO. OF ITEMS ? ";N        16:   G(1)=L/M
 5:   DIM M(N),L(N),V(N),G(2)          17:   G(2)=V/M
 6:   M=Ø:L=Ø:V=Ø                      18:   PAUSE "TOTAL MASS = "
 7:   FOR I=1 TO N                     19:   PRINT M
 8:   PAUSE "ITEM ";I                  2Ø:   PAUSE "OVERALL LCG = "
 9:   INPUT "MASS ? ";M(I)             21:   PRINT G(1)
1Ø:   INPUT "LCG ? ";L(I)              22:   PAUSE "OVERALL VCG = "
11:   INPUT "VCG ? ";V(I)              23:   PRINT G(2)
12:   M=M+M(I)                         24:   END
```

*Fig 171   Program in BASIC to calculate mass, LCG and VCG (limited to about 30 items on a
pocket computer, depending on the memory available and in use).*

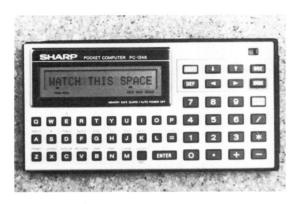

Fig 172   The program will run on a pocket computer of this kind, which is of relatively low cost.

Suppose we wish to find a first estimate of the volume of displacement of the yacht used as an example in the previous section. Assume a preliminary lines plan is available. We need to measure the length water-line and estimate the area of the largest section, perhaps by splitting it into simple shapes such as triangles or rectangles.

If the length water-line from the lines plan is 6.7m, and the area of the largest section is found to be 0.46m^2, the volume of the prism will be the product of 6.7m and 0.46m^2, that is 3.082m^2. If we judge the yacht's prismatic coefficient to be 0.56, that is to say that the actual volume of displacement is 56 per cent of the volume of the prism, then we predict a volume of displacement which is the product of the prism volume and the prismatic coeffi-

cient, which for this example equals 1.726m^3. It follows that displacement is $1.726 \times 1025 = 1769$kg, given that the yacht is destined for sea water rather than fresh.

No allowance has been made for the yacht's appendages. For a keel yacht, the volume of the keel is sufficient to be worthy of inclusion, even in the preliminary estimate. A cast-iron keel is likely to have a volume, and therefore displacement, 4 to 5 per cent that of the hull's displacement, while lead, being a more dense material, provides a relative volume of about 3 to 4 per cent. The rudder for a keel yacht is less significant, having a relative volume of about ½ per cent. The propeller bits and pieces can be regarded as a negligible displacement.

Making an allowance of, say, 4 per cent to allow for the keel and rudder, the displacement of the yacht becomes 1840kg. The difference between the estimates of displacement and mass (which was 1690kg) is 150kg. This probably is close enough at this preliminary stage, but it does depend upon the completeness of the mass estimate. Since stores, fuel or water were not included, it is reasonable that these would accommodate the 150kg difference.

If the difference is too great, then it is back to the drawing board in order to revise the underwater volume. The process does tend to be a trial and error one.

It has to be said that the paranoia which exists about the calculation of the mass, dis-

---

SUMMARY — ESTIMATES OF DISPLACEMENT

1   A preliminary estimate of the volume of displacement can be obtained by assuming a typical value of prismatic coefficient (0.5 to 0.65 for different hull types), from which the displacement can be calculated.

2   Allowance for the displacement of appendages may need to be made (for example of 3 to 5 per cent for a yacht's keel).

placement and water-line position of larger craft can be side-stepped for dinghies. The mass of the crew varies as people vary, and fore and aft trim can be changed by crew position. Such variables lessen the need for exactitude.

Areas and Centres of Gravity

For a preliminary estimate of displacement, crude methods for finding the area of the midship's section suffice. However, more accuracy requires greater sophistication.

Although we can draw the section or half-section on graph paper and count the squares enclosed, this is only accurate if we use the small squares, and then it takes a boringly long time. A better system is required which offers a standard set of simple instructions having a numerical basis (known as an *algorithm*) so that the brain can be slipped into cruising mode. Fundamentally, such systems rest upon simplifying the totalling of the areas of regular shapes.

One possibility is shown in Fig 173. Each shape is a trapezium with a common width. We measure the length of all the parallel sides (called *ordinates*) and the *common interval*, CI, or spacing between ordinates. A little mathematical magic produces a simple formula, and a good but low estimate of the area of the half-section pops out of the hat.

Another trapezoidal possibility is shown in Fig 174. A wave of the mathematical wand and we have another formula for the area, which this time provides a high estimate of the true area. Those readers who are maths smart may spot that an average (in fact a weighted average) of the two formulae would produce a better estimate yet.

The resulting formula of interest is described by the name of the mathematician Thomas Simpson; hence we have *Simpson's rule* (not Tom's rule). An important assumption made by this rule is that the estimate of area is based upon a specific boundary. A *parabola* is assumed across successive sets of three ordinate points. A parabola can be described by the curve produced by a batten held down by weights located at the points (*see* Fig 175).

For most 'easy' curves, such as gently rounded sections or water-lines, the area

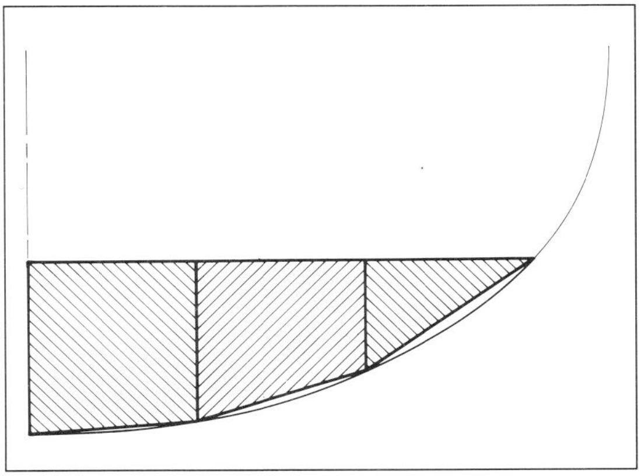

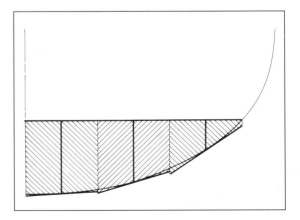

Fig 173   Based on trapezia, the rule measures the hatched area, thereby underestimating the true area for a convex curve.

Fig 174   When trapezia are constructed as shown, the area is overestimated, but again only for a convex curve.

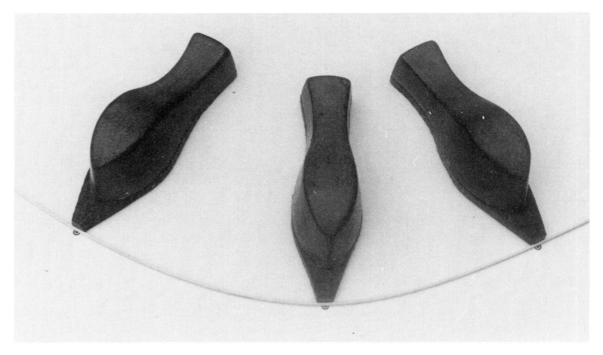

Fig 175   A parabola results from a parallel batten held at three points.

which they circumscribe can be determined accurately by Simpson's rule. However, finding the area of the lateral plane of a sailing yacht, as in Fig 176, is a misuse of the rule because the profile, including keel and rudder, is not well described by parabolas across triples of points. Separating the hull plane from the keel and rudder solves the problem.

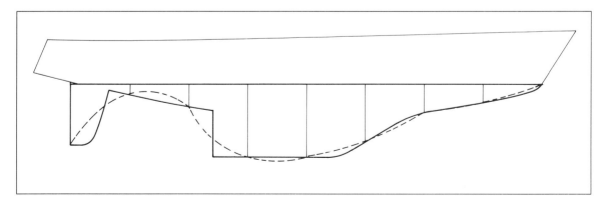

Fig 176   The series of dotted lines indicates the boundary of the area which Simpson's rule presumes.

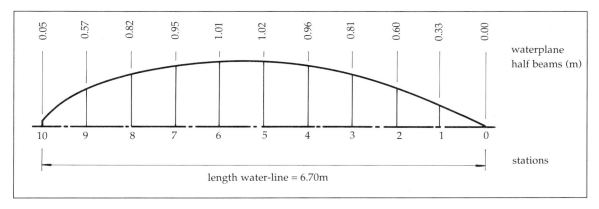

0.05 0.57 0.82 0.95 1.01 1.02 0.96 0.81 0.60 0.33 0.00

waterplane
half beams (m)

10   9   8   7   6   5   4   3   2   1   0

stations

length water-line = 6.70m

Fig 177   Offsets for the half waterplane of the small yacht depicted in Fig 170.

The procedure used to determine the area of a figure bounded by a curve is as follows:

1   Divide a base line into an equal number of spaces, that is an odd number of divisions. More divisions mean more accuracy, less mean less sweat.
2   Construct ordinates at each division perpendicularly to the base line.
3   Check that the curve is adequately close to a parabola across each set of three points.
4   Measure the length from the base line to the curve for each ordinate.
5   Measure the common interval of the ordinates. It is best to measure the total length and divide by the number of spaces.
6   The finale. Apply Simpson's rule. It usually is best to tabulate the numbers.

An example of the use of Simpson's rule, in finding the area of a half-waterplane, demonstrates the method (*see* Figs 177 and 178).

Simpson's multipliers follow a pattern: for three ordinates the multipliers are 1,4,1; for five ordinates 1,4,2,4,1; and generally the multipliers are 1,4,2,4, . . . 2,4,1.

A computer program to calculate area using Simpson's rule is listed (*see* Fig 179). The number of ordinates, their lengths and the base line length must be input and, after the computer has done its stuff, the area is displayed. The line numbers commence from 3∅ so that this program and the one previously presented to calculate mass can both be saved on a pocket computer.

Calculations of area based on the lines plan frequently crop up and a computer program speeds up a repetitive process. Another fast but usually not so accurate a method of finding area is by using a planimeter (*see* Fig 180). The planimeter is run around the perimeter of the figure, the area then being read directly from the scale. A traditional piece of equipment, the planimeter has been superseded by hydrostatics programs just as the sextant has been displaced by GPS (Global Positioning System) or Decca for navigation.

Technology of an even more primitive kind is often used to establish the centroid of a figure; balancing a cut-out of the figure serves well. Again, computer techniques can also be applied, and these are normally rooted in taking moments of the increments of the area. Simpson's rule forms the basis of the method. The example for the half-waterplane serves to demonstrate the approach. Moments (in fact,

Station number	A Ordinates (half waterplane beams)	B Simpson's multipliers	A × B Functions of ordinates
0	0.00	1	0.00
1	0.33	4	1.32
2	0.60	2	1.20
3	0.81	4	3.24
4	0.96	2	1.92
5	1.02	4	4.08
6	1.01	2	2.02
7	0.95	4	3.80
8	0.82	2	1.64
9	0.57	4	2.28
10	0.05	1	0.05
		Sum of functions of ordinates =	21.55

Length water-line $= 6.70$m

which implies that CI $= \dfrac{6.7}{10} = 0.67$m

The area is given by A $= \dfrac{CI}{3} \times$ (sum of functions of ordinates)

$= \dfrac{0.67}{3} \times (21.55)$

$= 4.81$m^2.

Therefore the total waterplane area $A_{WP} = 4.81 \times 2$

$= $ **9.62**m^2.

Fig 178   Calculation of the area of a waterplane.

```
30:  PAUSE "AREA CALCULATION"        39:  T=Ø
31:  PAUSE "(SIMPSONS RULE)"         40:  FOR I=2 TO (N-1) STEP 2
32:  INPUT "COM.INTERVAL? ";S        41:  T=T+L(I-1)+4*L(I)+L(I+1)
33:  INPUT "NO.ORDINATES? ";N        42:  NEXT I
34:  DIM L(N)                        43:  A=S/3*T
35:  FOR I=1 TO N                    44:  PAUSE "AREA = "
36:  PAUSE "NO. ";I                  45:  PRINT A
37:  INPUT "ORD.LENGTH? ";L(I)       46:  END
38:  NEXT I
```

Fig 179   Program to calculate the area of a curved shape.

Fig 180 A planimeter.

levers, as they are termed, being multiples of the *CI* spacing) are taken from the right-hand end (station 0). The tabulation of the area calculation is extended to find the longitudinal centroid (*see* Fig 181).

Calculations Based on the Lines Plan

When the lines plan is completed, various calculations must be performed to check that the hull will float as expected, that is, so that

$A \times B$ Functions of ordinates	C Lever from Station 0	$(A \times B) \times C$ Functions of moments
0.00	0	0.00
1.32	1	1.32
1.20	2	2.40
3.24	3	9.72
1.92	4	7.68
4.08	5	20.40
2.02	6	12.12
3.80	7	26.60
1.64	8	13.12
2.28	9	20.52
0.05	10	0.50
Sum of functions of ordinates = 21.55	Sum of functions of moments =	114.38

$$CI = 0.67$$

$$\text{Distance of centroid aft of station 0} = \frac{\text{Sum of functions of moments}}{\text{Sum of functions of ordinates}} \times CI$$

$$= \frac{114.38}{21.55} \times 0.67$$

$$= 3.56\text{m.}$$

The centroid therefore is positioned **3.56m** aft of station 0 (the forward ending of the water-line).

Fig 181 Extension of the area calculation to find the longitudinal centroid of the half-waterplane.

SUMMARY — AREAS AND CENTRES OF GRAVITY

1 The area of a figure bounded by a curve can be found by (a) square counting; (b) using a planimeter; (c) using numerical rules such as the trapezoidal or Simpson's rule.

2 Simpson's rule usually provides an accurate algorithm, which takes the form:
$$\text{area} = \frac{CI}{3} \times \{a + (4 \times b) + (2 \times c) + (4 \times d) \ldots (2 \times x) + (4 \times y)\}$$
where a, b, c . . . are ordinate lengths.

3 The centroid of a curved figure can be found by taking moments (for simplicity, levers are used, being multiples of the CI). The centroid position is given by:
$$\text{distance} = \frac{\text{sum of functions of moments}}{\text{sum of functions of ordinates}} \times CI$$

---

water isn't lapping the decks, the bow isn't under the water, the rudder isn't out of the water and the boat floats the right way up. Of first importance is the volume of displacement, which at this stage must be calculated with some accuracy.

The approach often adopted is by drawing a *curve of sectional areas* which also provides another check on the fairness of the lines plan. The curve of sectional areas, or just curve of areas, is no more than a graph with the area of each section up to the design water-line scaled on one axis, and the length water-line on the other (*see* Fig 182). But in some circles, a mystique has surrounded the shape of this curve, some designers believing that its shape should take on, in parts, the natural form of waves. If one starts from a pre-determined general shape for the curve of areas, this serves as a starting point in drawing the hull lines, though normally the curve follows rather than precedes the lines plan.

Referring to Fig 183, the volume of a transverse slice of the underwater volume is given by the product of the area of the section and the thickness of the slice. The volume of this slice is seen to be represented by the *area* of

the rectangle shown in the curve of areas. Continuing this reasoning for the complete length water-line, and using very thin slices, it follows that the volume of displacement is given by the area of the curve of areas.

A planimeter can be brought into play (or in to play with). Trundle it around the curve of areas, make allowance for its scale (the difficult part) and we obtain its area, that is, the boat's underwater volume. The alternative is to apply Simpson's rule where each sectional area is represented by an ordinate, and the common interval is the station spacing. This is why, conventionally, eleven stations are used; don't forget that Simpson's rule requires an odd number of ordinates. The method is the same as was presented for finding the area of curved shapes on page 153 (in this case, the 'ordinate length' becomes an area).

While playing with the curve of sectional areas, it makes sense to balance a cut-out of its shape, or take moments, as described previously, to find its centre of gravity position along the water-line. This position is the longitudinal centre of buoyancy for the hull.

For both the volume of displacement and

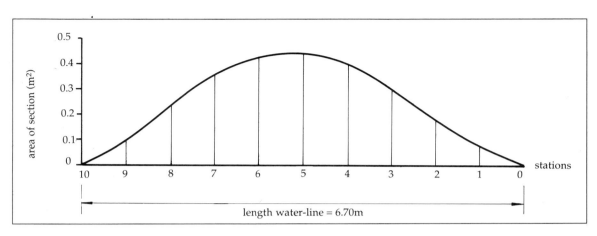

Fig 182   The shape of the curve of areas is basically the same as the water pressure distribution (Fig 167) expressed in terms of vertical components of force.

the longitudinal centre of buoyancy, allowance must be made for the keel and rudder volumes. These generally are not allowed for on the curve of sectional areas because Simpson's rule does not approve of the blips they produce on the curve, particularly for fin-

keeled types which are bound to produce undue error in the volume and centre of buoyancy calculations. Planimeters are much more tolerant.

Next comes the displacement, mass and centre of gravity calculation ritual. If you have

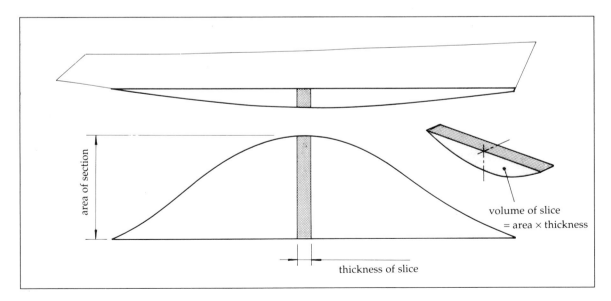

Fig 183   The representation of the volume of displacement.

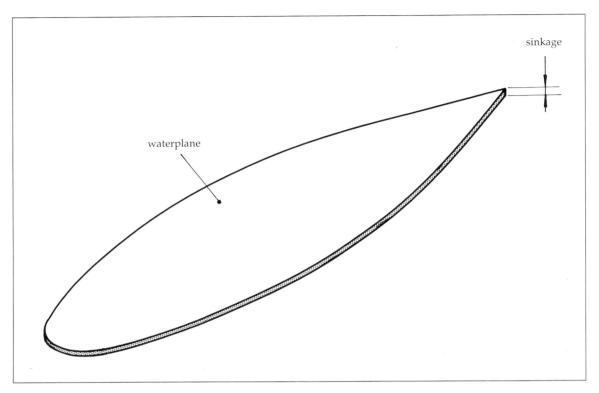

Fig 184   *The slice of water is regarded to be a prism for which the cross-section is the waterplane area and the length is the sinkage.*

been working through a practical example and using this text in cookbook style, you will need to use a lines plan, construction plan and general arrangement plan for these calculations. These final calculations take a long time. Next, you must blow off the dust from this cookbook and, unless you are very lucky, proceed with adjustments towards a match between the displacement and the mass.

Minor disagreement between the displacement and mass can usually be accommodated by a calculated vertical shift of the water-line. It also is useful to calculate how much sinkage would result from the addition (or removal) of ballast or stores or whatever. The approach is the same in both cases, Archimedes again having a contribution to make.

From Archimedes' principle, the mass of additional water displaced must equal the mass added, or the additional mass which must be accommodated. For a reasonably small sinkage, the volume of the horizontal slice of additional water displaced is given by the product of the area of the waterplane A_{WP} at the design water-line and the sinkage s (*see* Fig 184). The water's mass is given by the product of its volume and density ρ, for which sea water usually is presumed. Thus:

$$\text{mass} = A_{WP} \times s \times \rho.$$

Sinkage is therefore given by:

$$s = \frac{\text{change in displacement}}{A_{WP} \times \rho}$$

For example, the hypothetical sailing yacht of the last two chapters has a displacement of 1840kg and a mass of 1690kg on a waterplane area of 9.62m². The water-line would have to be lowered by:

$$s = \frac{(1840 - 1690)}{9.62 \times 1025} = 0.015m$$

i.e. 15mm for the displacement to match the mass.

Trim adjustments often have to be made where the centre of gravity of the mass of the construction and all the bits and pieces does not align with the longitudinal centre of buoyancy. Either the water-line can be tilted slightly, for example up at the bow and down at the stern, or some repositioning of ballast or equipment can be made.

Assuming the immersion of the bow is equal to the emersion of the stern, or vice versa, approximately (actually very approximately) the immersion/emersion t is given by one-third of the product of the mass moved and the distance through which it is moved divided by the boat's mass. For instance, an engine of 150kg moved 2m forward on our hypothetical yacht of 1690kg mass reduces freeboard forward (and increases it aft) by:

$$t = \frac{1}{3} \times \frac{150 \times 2}{1690}$$
$$= 0.059m \ (59mm)$$

If the boat's mass does not align with the longitudinal centre of buoyancy, the same formula can be used. In this case, the mass moved happens to be the boat itself, and this simplifies the formula to one-third of the misalignment. For example, if the centre of gravity calculation places the mass 0.06m forward of the longitudinal centre of buoyancy, the immersion/emersion will be:

$$t = \frac{1}{3} \times 0.06 = 0.20m \ (20mm)$$

This formula only approximates to the trim change. It is inexact because no account is made of hull form. If a boat is of beamy, heavy displacement form, the one-third multiplier could be replaced by one-half. Ultra-light displacement types (towards featherlight) and multihulls would get their trims adjusted more accurately by using a factor of one-fifth.

The last significant calculation based on the lines plan which needs to be made is the vertical location of the centre of buoyancy. (It helps to think of the centre of buoyancy as the centre of gravity of the displaced water – imagine it to be a block of ice.) The *vertical centre of buoyancy*, as it is termed, is calculated because it has an important bearing on stability.

In principle, the calculation of the vertical centre of buoyancy is approached in exactly the same manner as is the longitudinal centre of buoyancy, except that moments of the waterplane are used rather than sections. This does require, for Simpson's rule to be used directly, that the hull draught is divided into an even number of spaces. Moments, or 'levers' as used for LCB, can be taken either from the design water-line, the bottom of the hull or keel, or a base line.

If the water-lines do not suitably divide the hull draught, a *curve of waterplane areas* can be drawn (*see* Fig 185) and if patience is running out, this can be balanced. The alternative is to erase the waterplane areas on the curve and draw a new set of ordinates, equally spaced and odd in number. Simpson's rule can now be used.

A good approximation to the vertical centre of buoyancy is given by Morrish's formula, which indicates that the distance of the centre of buoyancy below the design water-line is:

$$VCB = \frac{1}{3} \times \left(\frac{H}{2} + \frac{V}{A_{WP}} \right)$$

where H is the hull draught, V is the volume of displacement and A_{WP} is the area of the waterplane as before. This formula relates to the hull only, and it is important that the

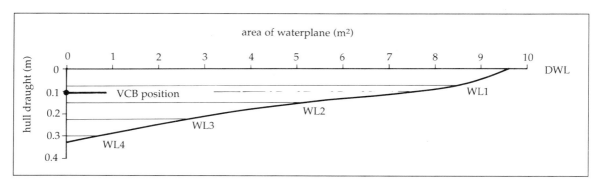

Fig 185   The curve of waterplane areas. Its area also represents the volume of displacement.

buoyancies of the keel and rudder are allowed for by taking moments. The approach adopted is by taking moments from a datum, such as a point on the design water-line, of the volumes of the hull, keel and rudder. The relevant distances are measured vertically from the datum to the respective centres of buoyancy, just as for the VCG calculation.

Few other calculations from the lines plan are a real must. Prismatic coefficient and wet-ted surface area (obtained with a little adaptation using Simpson's rule) are useful for comparative and performance purposes, but the real trick about the lines plan calculations is not to do it if you can't use it, and to judge how accurate the answers you do need must be, and go no further than is necessary. There is a tendency to Simpsonize absolutely everything on the lines plan with the exception of the title block.

SUMMARY — CALCULATIONS BASED ON THE LINES PLANS

1   The volume of displacement is given by the area of the curve of sectional areas and can be found using Simpson's rule. The fin keel and rudder are calculated separately.

2   Vertical changes to the water-line, or the sinkage resulting from ballasting, are given by:

$$s = \frac{\text{change in displacement}}{A_{\text{WP}} \times \rho}$$

3   Trim changes are given approximately by:

$$t = \frac{1}{3} \times \frac{(\text{mass moved} \times \text{distance})}{\text{boat's mass}}$$

The multiplier would be adapted for different hull forms. The trim resulting from LCG and LCB misalignment is given by one-third of the horizontal distance between LCG and LCB.

4   VCB is found by taking moments as for LCB (or by balancing the curve of waterplane areas). Alternatively, Morrish's formula provides an approximation:

$$\text{VCB below DWL} = \frac{1}{3} \times \left(\frac{H}{2} + \frac{\nabla}{A_{\text{WP}}} \right)$$

Chapter 6

Design Procedures

There are design procedures, and then there are design procedures. Some are more complex than others according to the size or type of boat, but the designer's own style plays a part. To adopt too rigid an approach can be constraining.

Perhaps the first stage should be the three Rs – Reading, Researching and Reflecting – in order to come to an understanding of the context of small craft design. But I think the direction these take should be general. If one sets out to design a particular type of boat, reference to other successful designs of the same type tends to channel the mind, and this blots out other ideas and possibilities. Although it does make sense to look at the solutions which other designers have found, I would suggest that this should be done only when well along the path, and only as a check.

Design, whether of a deck or a Docksider, is a problem-solving activity. The problem is outlined in the form of a *design brief*, which is an expression of the target or the requirement of the design.

> . . . High-performance keelboat/cruiser – 8.5m length overall. Accommodation to meet very basic requirements only. Suitable for fast sailing/club racing/limited 'cruising'. Moderate to high ballast ratio. Two to five person crew. One-off construction to serve as a prototype for a production series.

As a guideline, the design should be tackled at three levels of increasing refinement. This avoids the mistake in design of becoming trapped in detail or of developing one area to the exclusion of another, only to find later in the procedure that incompatibility exists.

At the first level, all or most of the considerations for design are examined, if crudely. Various sketches of design ideas, including alternative options and very basic calculations or estimates, are made. There is no particular order in which these design sketches need to be carried out, though an outboard profile would probably be the starting point.

Fig 186 demonstrates the approach at this first level, based upon the design brief outlined above. At its most crude, this is a back-of-an-old-envelope approach, but more accuracy and greater speed are possible if graph paper is used. The graph paper should be of the feint-lined variety so that the grid does not dominate, making it more difficult to appreciate the form being worked on. As part of the process, it may help to make a photocopy; if the contrast is set correctly the grid will not be printed.

These early sketches should not be too large as this tends to inhibit visualization of the form. One approach is to work all sketches, calculations and estimates on a single sheet of paper no larger than A3 size. But the sketches should be to scale, though recognized scales such as 1:100 or 1:50 are not necessary. It often is convenient to create one's own scale (for instance 1 in:2m, or 1cm:1ft), a scale rule being created from a strip of card.

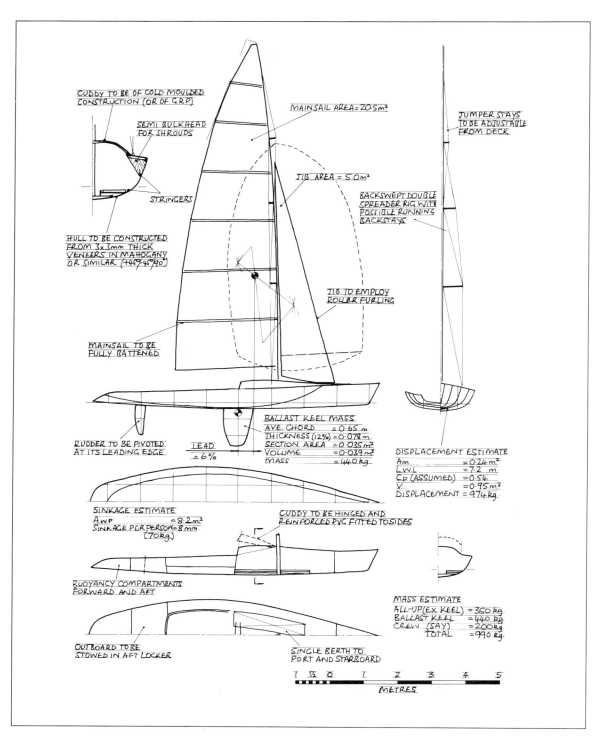

CUDDY TO BE OF COLD MOULDED
CONSTRUCTION (OR OF G.R.P.)

SEMI BULKHEAD
FOR SHROUDS

STRINGERS

HULL TO BE CONSTRUCTED
FROM 3x3mm THICK
VENEERS IN MAHOGANY
OR SIMILAR (+45°/45°/90°)

MAINSAIL TO BE
FULLY BATTENED

RUDDER TO BE PIVOTED
AT ITS LEADING EDGE

SINKAGE ESTIMATE
AWP   = 8.2 m²
SINKAGE PER PERSON = 8 mm.
(70 kg.)

BUOYANCY COMPARTMENTS
FORWARD AND AFT

OUTBOARD TO BE
STOWED IN AFT LOCKER

MAINSAIL AREA = 20.5 m²

JIB AREA = 5.0 m²

JIB TO EMPLOY
ROLLER FURLING

LEAD
= 6%

BALLAST KEEL MASS
AVE. CHORD   = 0.65 m.
THICKNESS (12%) = 0.078 m.
SECTION AREA   = 0.035 m²
VOLUME   = 0.039 m³
MASS   = 44.0 kg.

CUDDY TO BE HINGED AND
REINFORCED PVC FITTED TO SIDES

SINGLE BERTH TO
PORT AND STARBOARD

JUMPER STAYS
TO BE ADJUSTABLE
FROM DECK

BACKSWEPT DOUBLE
SPREADER RIG WITH
POSSIBLE RUNNING
BACKSTAYS

DISPLACEMENT ESTIMATE
Am   = 0.24 m²
L.W.L   = 7.2 m.
Cp (ASSUMED)   = 0.54
V   = 0.95 m³
DISPLACEMENT = 974 kg.

MASS ESTIMATE
ALL-UP (EX KEEL) = 350 kg
BALLAST KEEL   = 440 kg
CREW (SAY)   = 200 kg.
TOTAL   = 990 kg.

I 1½ 0   I   2   3   4   5
METRES

Fig 186   A quickly completed sketch outline based upon the design brief.

162

Sketching to scale helps the next level, which involves firming up on the ideas already propagated. Before the next level is started in earnest, it may well help to make some check against existing designs or recommendations from various sources in the hope that this will verify one's thinking up to that point, or at least expose some ghastly error of judgement. But design needs commitment and one should not be swayed too easily. If breaking new ground, there is a sense of being on one's own, though there are bound to be points of reference out there.

I suggest the following procedure for level two, but must emphasize that this is a personal choice. Certain stages must precede others, but for many there is no immutable order.

1   Draw, with reasonable accuracy, a preliminary lines plan including appendages on a basic grid (use graph paper). It is not necessary to divide the water-line length with eleven stations but they should be of equal spacing. Use an appropriate scale to give a profile length of about 250–300mm (10–12in).

2   Construct a curve of areas. Assign ordinates (an odd number) so that Simpson's rule can be used. Calculate the volume of displacement and the longitudinal centre of buoyancy.

3   Calculate the volumes of the appendages, which can be drawn to a larger scale, and hence find the overall displacement and longitudinal centre of buoyancy.

4   Complete the other lines plan calculations, such as the vertical centre of buoyancy, the prismatic coefficient and the position of the metacentre.

5   Draw the sail plan to include all sails. Determine the centroid of the sail plan and of the underwater profile (or consider the centres of effort and lateral resistance). Check the lead, making adjustments to the sail plan and keel or centreboard if necessary.

6   Draw a general arrangement of the accommodation, the superstructure and the cockpit.

Include the engine, steering gear, equipment and other such items.

7   Draw a construction plan, specifying the dimensions of the materials to be used. For GRP (glass-reinforced plastic), the thickness or weight per square metre of the lay-up would be specified.

8   Draw the rigging layout and deck layout to include the principal winches and deck hardware and the lead of the running rigging and control lines.

9   Undertake reasonably detailed mass, longitudinal and vertical centre of gravity calculations. Make allowance for variable loadings such as fuel, water and crew.

10   Cross fingers. Check for closeness of mass and displacement, and of longitudinal centre of gravity and longitudinal centre of buoyancy.

11   Check that stability is satisfactory. Possibly examine power to carry sail to ensure that an appropriate sail area is proposed.

Obviously, the list would be amended for different types of craft, some items being omitted, some added. Much could be completed using a computer.

A rather more thorough review of other similar craft for comparison might be made at this stage. This is often accomplished by producing a *data plot* of principal dimensions, chosen to reflect performance or seaworthiness, of a number of craft of a similar size.

For example, a graph comprising plotted data can be constructed based on beam and length. Several designs of the same type of craft are chosen and the data entered on a graph. This indicates a trend, and an 'average' beam for a particular length can be determined from the graph.

Another way in which information can be expressed is in the form of a ratio. For example, the length:beam ratio for a catamaran typically might be 2:1. A ratio of length water-line to displacement provides an indicator of performance since the longer and lighter a boat is, the faster it is likely to be. Generally this is expressed as:

$$\frac{LWL}{\sqrt[3]{V}}$$

where LWL is the length water-line and V the volume of displacement. This expression is symbolized by *circular M*, $\text{\small Ⓜ}$. The keelboat-cum-cruiser to the design brief outlined has an $\text{\small Ⓜ}$ of about 7.3 which indicates a healthy planing performance. It is to be noted that the volume of displacement is not used directly; using the cubed root 'linearizes' this dimension so that the ratio is applicable to a range of craft of differing length.

As far as powering is concerned, the ratio of the power of the engine to the displacement assesses performance (though it is to be noted that this expression is defined by units of kW/ tonne). For sailing craft, a similar measure of driving force to resistance is given by:

$$\frac{\sqrt[2]{SA}}{\sqrt[3]{V}}$$

where SA is the sail area and V the volume of displacement. For the cruising keelboat this calculates to be about 5.1 which also indicates that it should be a healthy performer.

Model testing offers a more accurate system for predicting performance than using somewhat arbitrary performance ratios. Although few hulls are tank tested (and fewer sail plans treated to a wind tunnel or propellers to a water tunnel) this is a possible step in the design procedure.

When happy/convinced that the design should work/set the world alight, the time has come to move on to level three. This stage involves producing the accurate, fully sorted, all singing, all dancing, working drawings and calculations. In the main this is a replay of level two, though not an instant one!

Each plan is worked through methodically using a drawing pen and ink or a pencil, to choice. The task requires draughting skill; the body of the design work will have been completed before this stage. Each of the drawings is produced with sufficient information for the boat to be built, the engine to be fitted, the sails to be cut, the mast to be rigged and so on. Some detail drawings may be required, and an offset table is prepared from the lines plan.

If a computer and its attendant draughting

SUMMARY — DESIGN PROCEDURES

1   The starting point for a design is the design brief. From this point it is suggested that the design should be progressed at three levels of increasing refinement.

2   At the first level, initial ideas and possible solutions are sketched, based on the general considerations arising from the design brief. Various estimates are made, for example of displacement and mass.

3   The next level involves the selection and firming up of the ideas considered. Checks may be made against existing designs using data plots and linearized ratios such as $\text{\small Ⓜ}$. Reference to research organizations and other bodies may be warranted. Model testing may be undertaken.

4   Level three involves the creation of full working drawings, calculations and an offset table. Computers prove a valuable tool at this stage and perhaps at earlier levels, but should not rule the design work.

and hydrostatics software are used, the same basic procedure should still be adopted. Because modifications can be made and stored relatively easily, each plan can be developed as required on the screen. Using a plotter, the final drawings are produced, thus keeping the builders happy.

Some designers prefer to progress a design in a different order, and some find a three-layered iterative approach excessive. Although a mechanical procedure may make it appear so, small-craft design is not a simple step-by-step process. Design starts with the understanding of the principles combined with an ability to think creatively and analytically.

Computers for drawing and calculation work have become almost indispensable, but they should be used as tools rather than to replace fertile minds. Computers help the designer to design more effectively in the same way that a fast sailing boat realizes good helmsmanship. But computers don't design any more than fast boats sail themselves.

Helpful Conversion Factors

Numbers substituted into the formulae in this book must be in SI units (Système International d'Unités). These units are: metres (m); seconds (s); kilograms (kg); newtons (N); watts (W).

Measured	Measured in	. . . is equivalent to . . .	Approximate equivalent
Distance and length	metres (m) SI	1m 3.28ft	Multiply by three and a bit
		1m 39.4in	Multiply by forty
		1m 1.09yd	About equal
		1ft 0.305m	A bit less than one third
	millimetres (mm)	1mm . . . . 39.4 thou	Multiply by forty
		1in 25.4mm	Multiply by twenty five
		1m 1000mm	Multiply by one thousand (exact)
Area	metres squared or square metres (m²) SI	1m² 10.76ft²	Nearly eleven times
		1ft² 0.093m²	One tenth or one eleventh
Volume	metres cubed or cubic metres (m³) SI	1m³ 35.31ft	Multiply by thirty five
Velocity (or speed) (The change in distance with time)	metres per second (m/s) SI	1m/s . . . . 1.94 knots	Double
		1m/s 2.23mph	Multiply by two and a bit
		1 knot 0.515m/s	Halve
Acceleration (The change in velocity with time)	metres per second per second (m/s²) SI	1m/s² 3.28ft/s²	Multiply by three and a bit
Mass	kilograms (kg) SI	1kg 2.205lb	Double and add on one tenth of the result (e.g. 15kg → 15 × 2 → 30 → 30 + $\frac{30}{10}$ → 33lb)
		1kg 35.3oz	Multiply by thirty five
		1lb 0.456kg	Just under one half
	tonnes	1 tonne 1000kg	Multiply by one thousand (exact)
		1 tonne . . . . 0.984 ton	About equal
Density (The mass per unit volume)	kilograms per metre cubed (kg/m³) SI	1kg/m² 0.624lb/ft²	Don't bother trying!
		1lb/ft³ 16.02kg/m³	Multiply by sixteen
		1 tonne/m³ 1000kg/m³	Multiply by one thousand (exact)

Measured	Measured in	. . . is equivalent to . . .	Approximate equivalent
Force and Weight (The product of mass acceleration due to gravity	newtons (N) SI kilonewtons (kN)	1N . . . . 0.225lb 1N . . . . 3.6oz 1lb . . . . 4.45N 1kg . . . . 9.81N 1kN . . . . 1000N 1 ton 9.97kN	Slightly less than one quarter Multiply by three or four Multiply by four and a half Multiply by ten Multiply by one thousand (exact) Multiply by ten
Pressure (The force per unit area)	newtons per metre squared (often termed a pascal (Pa)) (N/m^2) SI	$1lb/in^2$ . . . . . . $6895N/m^2$ $101300N/m^2$ . . . . 1 atmosphere	Multiply by seven thousand Multiply by one hundred thousand
Power (The product of force and velocity)	watts (W) SI kilowatts (kW)	746W . . . . 1HP 1kW . . . . 1000W 1HP . . . . 0.746kW 1kW 1.34HP	Divide by seven or eight hundred Multiply by one thousand (exact) About three quarters Multiply by one and a third

Glossary

Advance The actual progression of a propeller in one revolution.

Aero- Relating to air.

Air resistance The resistance of all parts of the craft above the water.

Ambient flow The general rather than the local flow.

Angle of attack The angle at which a foil is presented to the ambient fluid flow.

Angle of deadrise The angle which each half of the hull bottom (usually of a planing craft) makes with the horizontal.

Appendage An underwater extension to the hull, such as the keel, rudder or propeller bracketry.

Appendage resistance The resistance of appendages.

Aspect ratio The ratio of the dimension of a foil measured perpendicularly to the fluid flow to the average chord length.

BASIC A simple computer language.

Body Any three-dimensional shape.

Body plan A plan on the lines plan depicting the sections of the hull.

Bow and buttock lines The outlines of vertical cutting planes parallel to the centreline plane depicted on the lines plan.

Camber The degree of asymmetry of a foil.

Cavitation Bubble formation resulting from extremely low pressure on a foil at high speed, which may lead to erosion damage.

Centre of buoyancy The centre of gravity of the displaced water.

Centre of effort The centre of the aerodynamic force of the sail plan.

Centre of force The point at which all forces could be considered to be acting (or the centre of gravity of the force distribution).

Centre of gravity The fixed point at which all the weight of a body could be considered to be acting whatever the position of the body.

Centre of lateral resistance The longitudinal position of the hydrodynamic force of the underwater surface of a sailing craft.

Characteristic length A length criterion used in Reynolds number.

Chord The straight line joining the leading and trailing edges of a foil, usually in the line of the fluid flow. The chord length is the length of this line.

Coefficient of drag A measure of streamlining. More correctly, the ratio of drag to ($\frac{1}{2} \times \rho \times a \times v^2$).

Coefficient of lift A measure of the efficiency of a foil in producing lift. More correctly, the ratio of lift to ($\frac{1}{2} \times \rho \times a \times v^2$).

Common interval The distance between regularly spaced lines, such as stations, used for calculating area.

Curve of sectional areas A curve of the areas of the sections on a base line of length water-line.

Data plot A graph on which is plotted one principal dimension against another for a variety of craft.

Design brief The outline specification for a design.

Design water-line The water-line at which a craft is expected to float.

Diagonal The outline of a cutting plane at an angle to the centreline plane depicted on the lines plan.

Directional stability The tendency for a craft to follow a straight course without helm correction.

Displacement The mass of water displaced by a boat.

Displacement hull form A hull form which is deep bodied and will not plane.

Divergent waves Waves formed which leave the hull at a consistent angle.

Drag The force or component of force in the line of the ambient fluid flow which results when a fluid flows past a body.

Drag line The line through which all drag can be considered to act.

Driving force The force or component of force pushing the craft in the direction of its course.

Dynamical similarity The similarity of flow conditions for both the model and the full-sized form.

Dynamics Relating to movement.

Eddy A zone where flow is reversed and generally disturbed.

Eddymaking resistance The resistance resulting from the production of eddies around the hull.

Electrical analogue technique A means of predicting streamlines based on electrical potential deemed analogous to pressure differential.

Empirical Found by experiment.

Fence An obstruction attached perpendicularly to the surface of a rudder in line with the water flow to minimize ventilation.

Fluids Gases and liquids having the property of flowing.

Foil A lift device.

Form drag The drag resulting from a fully immersed body's form or shape exclusive of frictional drag.

Frictional drag The drag resulting from a fluid in contact with and flowing past a surface.

Froude number A criterion, based on the wave system, providing a measure of the velocity of a hull relative to its water-line length.

Half angle of entrance The angle between the water-line and the centreline in plan.

Half breadth plan A plan on the lines plan depicting the sheerline, water-lines and level lines.

Heaving The rising bodily of the hull.

Heeling force The force, or component of force, heeling a sailing craft.

Heeling resistance The additional resistance resulting from heeling.

Hogged sheer A sheerline which rises in the middle relative to the ends. Sometimes called a reverse sheer.

Hump speed The speed at which a significant increase in resistance occurs, producing a bulge in the resistance–speed curve.

Hydro- Relating to water.

Ideal fluid A theoretical fluid for which there is no friction against a surface or within itself, and for which no wake is formed.

Induced resistance The resistance resulting from the production of a lift force.

Kinematic viscosity The ratio of a fluid's viscosity to its density.

Kinetic energy Energy resulting from movement.

Knuckle An overhanging ledge running the length of the hull.

Laminar flow Fluid flow in which 'layers' of the fluid shear regularly one over the other with negligible transverse movement.

Lateral plane The profile plane of a craft below the water-line.

Lead The distance, often expressed as a percentage of the water-line length, by which the sail centroid lies ahead of the centroid of the lateral plane.

Lee helm The helm required to counteract the tendency for a sailing craft to turn away from the wind.

Leeward Away from the wind.

Leeway Sideways drift, usually of sailing craft.

Level lines The outlines of horizontal cutting planes above the design water-line depicted on the lines plan.

Levers A means of assessing distance, measured in terms of multiples of the common interval, to simplify taking moments in area and centre of gravity calculations.

Lift The force, or component of force, perpendicular to the ambient fluid flow which results when a fluid flows past a body.

Lift-drag ratio The ratio of lift to drag (or the coefficient of lift to the coefficient of drag).

Lines The outlines of the cutting planes considered in the design of the hull and presented on the lines plan.

Lofting The drawing of the lines plan on a loft floor at full size to improve the fairness of the lines and the accuracy of the offsets.

Longitudinal centre of buoyancy The longitudinal position of the centre of gravity of the displaced water.

Mathematical modelling Expressing a real situation or problem in (usually) a mathematical and simplified way, such that satisfactory predictions can be made.

Maximum displacement speed The reasonable maximum speed which a displacement craft can reach.

Metacentre The intersection of the centreline and a vertical from the centre of buoyancy of the hull when heeled.

Metacentric height The distance between the centre of gravity and the metacentre.

Moment The product of a force and its perpendicular distance from a point.

Momentum Having the properties of both mass and velocity.

Normal Perpendicular to a surface.

Offsets The measurements, from a datum such as the centreline or design water-line, of all the lines.

Ordinate A straight line, perpendicular to an axis, which meets a curve. Usually refers to the length of the line.

Parabola (adj.:parabolic) A curve which has a defined curvature which changes progressively, as in the case of a non-tapered batten held at three points.

Pitch The theoretical progression of a propeller in one revolution, assuming that water is unyielding.

Pitching Rhythmical fore and aft oscillations of the hull.

Pitchpoling A craft capsizing end for end, usually in a following sea.

Planform The outline shape of a foil.

Planing The condition in which a craft's weight is supported in large part by the dynamic lift forces.

Potential energy Energy resulting from height.

Porpoising The hull's rhythmical leaping from or partly from the water with attendant trim changes, in the manner of a porpoise.

Pressure Force per unit area.

Prismatic coefficient The ratio of the volume of displacement to the product of the largest sectional area underwater and the length water-line.

Profile plan A plan on the lines plan depicting a craft's profile, or side view, and its bow and buttock lines.

Residual resistance The sum of all components of resistance with the exception of frictional resistance (and usually air resistance).

Reynolds number A criterion, based on

fluid flow conditions, usually providing a measure of velocity taking account of length, for a fluid flowing past a surface or a fully immersed body.

Section The outline of a cutting plane which for the hull is vertical and transverse, and for the keel or rudder is horizontal.

Separation A region of disturbance with some reverse flow of the fluid distinct and separate from the surface. It usually occurs towards the rear of a body.

Sheer The profile curvature of the sheerline.

Sheerline The line indicating the intersection of the topsides and the deck, its profile usually being referred to.

Simpson's rule A rule for making a good estimation of the area of a figure bounded by a curve.

Slip The difference between a propeller's pitch and its advance.

Spray rails Triangular sectioned strips running fore and aft on the hull, either attached to the surface or moulded in.

Stability curve A graph of stability against angle of heel.

Stagnation streamline The streamline which meets a body in such a way that it has no tendency to move to either side.

Stalling The total breakdown of flow on the low pressure surface of a foil.

Stations The location of the sections of the hull.

Streamline The path of a particle of a fluid.

Streamlined flow Theoretical flow of an ideal fluid.

Streamtube The theoretical tube within a fluid defined by two streamlines.

Surface frictional drag As for **Frictional drag**.

Total force The overall force produced by a foil.

Transom flaps Flaps attached to the bottom of the transom on planing craft. Sometimes termed 'trim tabs'.

Transverse waves Waves formed perpendicularly to the boat's centreline.

Trim The fore and aft attitude of the hull in the water. The angle of trim is the angle of the keel (usually for planing craft) to the water surface.

Turbulent flow The irregular shearing of 'layers' of a fluid when flowing over a surface.

Upthrust The upward force resulting on a static body in a fluid, otherwise known as buoyancy.

Ventilation The drawing of air on to the lower pressure surface of a foil immersed in water.

Venturi The narrowed section of a tube or channel.

Viscous pressure resistance The resistance from the viscous effects of a fluid.

Volume of displacement The volume of water displaced by a craft.

Vortex streets Swirling flow occurring behind a body.

Wake The eddying flow of a fluid behind a body in a fluid stream.

Water-lines The outlines of horizontal cutting planes below the design water-line depicted on the lines plan.

Waterplane The plane at a water-line, usually the design water-line, but can refer to any water-line.

Wavelength Distance between wave crests.

Wave-making resistance The resistance of the hull resulting from the production of a wave system.

Wave system The pattern of waves formed around the hull.

Weather helm The helm required to counteract the tendency for a sailing craft to turn towards the wind.

Index